COMPL EMENT

**The Surprising Beauty of Choosing
Together Over Separate in Marriage**

In true Aaron and Jamie style, this book is real, raw, hilarious, and full of wisdom. They do not sugar coat the challenges of marriage yet invite married couples to discover the beauty and adventure God has purposed for our marriages. We need this book in this time and culture.

Nick and Christine Caine, founders of A21

Today's culture often alludes to marriage as a monotonous, contractual agreement that can easily be undone and reversed. Aaron and Jamie have delightfully intertwined their firsthand experiences to expound upon God's deepest desires for marriage. This book is for every couple who wants to do the hard work and intentionally live out their covenant.

Gabe and Rebekah Lyons, bestselling authors and cofounders of Q Ideas

As in all of life, the best marriage mentors are the ones who not only have a compelling message, but also a compelling life to share. Our friends Aaron and Jamie Ivey are such mentors who offer us their marriage "message" through the lens of Scripture. For who can tell us more about healthy, life-giving marriage than the Maker of marriage Himself? As Aaron and Jamie take us on this journey, they do so in a way that reveals their own life together. In the sharing of their lives as an illustration of their message, they provide a compelling path for other husbands and wives to follow. We cannot recommend *Complement* highly enough!

Scott and Patti Sauls, Christ Presbyterian Church, Nashville, Tennessee

The Colliers believe that in marriage, if you're not having fun, you're doing something wrong. Aaron and Jamie are having the most fun and teaching couples how to press through the messy middles of marriage to create a continual flow of synergy, together. In this incredible book, the Iveys are showing us how to be who we each were created to be while leaning on the power of Jesus to help us draw nearer to our spouses for a life of connection, clarity, and screaming-at-the-top-of-our-lungs cheering for the one you share forever with.

Sam and Toni Collier, lead pastors of Hillsong Atlanta

As this book says, "No one stumbles into marriage. It has to be built." We can so relate to this, and we wish we had this book in our hands a decade ago! What Aaron and Jamie do in *Complement* is point us to a biblical perspective of marriage that is centered on the faithful work of Jesus. They dig deep into their own marriage and into the Bible to give us winsome and vital truth that comes to life and can be lived out every day. This isn't a book to be read "some day"; you should read it today. As you do, you're going to be challenged, encouraged, and filled with hope.

Joel and Brittany Muddamalle, Proverbs 31 Ministries | Transformation Church

COMPL EMENT

The Surprising Beauty of Choosing
Together Over Separate in Marriage

Jamie Ivey

B&H
PUBLISHING
NASHVILLE, TENNESSEE

978-1-5359-9669-3

Published by B&H Publishing Group
Nashville, Tennessee

Published in association with Jenni Burke of Illuminate
Literary Agency: www.illuminateliterary.com.

Dewey Decimal Classification: 306.81
Subject Heading: MARRIAGE / HUSBANDS / WIVES

Unless otherwise noted, all Scripture is taken from The Holy
Bible, English Standard Version. ESV® Text Edition: 2016.
Copyright © 2001 by Crossway Bibles, a publishing ministry
of Good News Publishers.

Also used: The Christian Standard Bible (csb), copyright
© 2017 by Holman Bible Publishers. Used by permission.
Christian Standard Bible®, and CSB® are federally registered
trademarks of Holman Bible Publishers, all rights reserved.

Cover design by B&H Publishing Group. Author photo by
Becca Matimba Photography @bmatimbaphoto. Texture by
HolyCrazyLazy/shutterstock.

It is the Publisher's goal to minimize disruption caused by tech-
nical errors or invalid websites. While all links are active at the
time of publication, because of the dynamic nature of the inter-
net, some web addresses or links contained in this book may
have changed and may no longer be valid. B&H Publishing
Group bears no responsibility for the continuity or content of
the external site, nor for that of subsequent links. Contact the
external site for answers to questions regarding its content.

1 2 3 4 5 6 • 25 24 23 22 21

To our children: Cayden, Amos, Deacon, and Story Ivey

If God has marriage in His plan for your life
(and it's okay if He doesn't), we pray your
marriage is fun, thrilling, Jesus-honoring, and always
complementing each other throughout life.

Contents

Preface

We're so glad you picked up this book! We wholeheartedly believe that marriage is one of God's incredible gifts to us as His children. While it's not the ultimate thing in life, marriage is meant to be life-giving, thrilling, and beautiful for those who experience it.

We've been through sweet times and difficult times in the two decades of our marriage, and through it all we've learned that God designed marriage to be a living picture of His great love for His people. It's hard. It takes a lot of work, forgiveness, patience, and time. But we've found it to be worth it. And we want you to as well.

In a culture where marriage can be viewed as bland, archaic, or boring, we've found a better way. And it isn't because we do it all correctly or have some special brand of marriage that is unattainable for some. As we've studied God's Word and seen more of His faithfulness in our own lives, we've actually come to see that God's purpose in marriage is more surprising and exciting than we realized.

We believe in marriage. We believe in *your* marriage. We want it to be healthy and vibrant, fueled by the love of Jesus, and a powerful tool of mission in the world in which we live.

In this book, you're getting two perspectives on the same themes. We took the most valuable things we've learned about complementing each other in marriage and wrote our unique perspectives on them. In fact, we didn't even read each other's portions of the book until in the late editing stages, so what you're getting is the raw, real, and vulnerable perspective on how we complement each other as we strive to honor Jesus with our marriage.

We'd encourage you to think of this not as two books, but two halves of the same book—and to read both halves. Read one half, then trade with your spouse. We think you'll find encouragement and challenges as you read both of our thoughts on each concept.

We're fighting for *your* marriage, even from a distance. It's an honor to join you on the journey of choosing together over separate in marriage.

Aaron and Jamie Ivey

What I Thought Marriage Would Be

'll never forget that day in the summer of 1999 when I walked into my dad's office as a young twenty-one-year-old bride-to-be, and said the words out loud that had been haunting me, suffocating me, for weeks.

"Dad," I said, "I don't think I can marry him."

Just in saying it, I felt as though a ginormous weight had been lifted off of my shoulders, even as I waited for my dad's reaction, wondering if he'd tell me I needed to figure out a way to make it work, or that I didn't have to go through with it. I expected my dad to take my side, which is why he'd been my first go-to. But I also knew plans had been made. People's time had been invested. Lots of money was involved. So I was nervous. He certainly, in my eyes, had every right to be really angry and frustrated with me.

Looking back though, I count that moment as a key indicator that I was finally growing up inside. I'd gotten cold feet, yes. I hadn't been able to shake the fact that I wasn't supposed to marry this man. But instead of pushing through and trying to figure things out on my own, I'd actually been listening to the Holy Spirit on this one. Which wasn't normal for me. And from the best I could tell, He was clearly showing me a way out. And I'd decided to follow Him through it.

Obviously, I hadn't gone into things at first with the intention of canceling an engagement and breaking someone's heart. I'd wanted it to work out. I'm never one who likes to admit I can't do something I set out to do. I hate letting people down, and with this one decision I felt like I was letting *everyone* down. A tug-of-war of the soul for sure, especially for a people-pleaser like me.

But Dad said he would support me in my decision, which confirmed it all for me. So I called off the wedding, sold the dress, my parents lost a bunch of deposits, and I started the process of sharing the news with family. I was sad about hurting a person that I really did love—as much as my heart could love anyone at that moment—but I can say I felt more confident about this decision than any other I'd ever made in my entire lifetime.

I recalled this story recently to someone and told them what I'm about to tell you. Making that decision to call off the wedding and break up with my fiancé was, and still is, one of the hardest things I've ever done. But I can also say in the same breath that it's one of the best things, if not *the* best thing (behind following Jesus, of course) that I have ever committed myself to doing. *Ever.* That twenty-one-year-old girl was way braver than she thought she was. As naive as I was, in terms of what marriage entailed and what it meant to truly love well, God had given me a healthy enough dose of knowledge about what marriage was meant to be that it kept me from walking into one that wasn't best for me.

Two years later I happily stood at the altar facing my one and only husband, Aaron, and committed myself to a lifetime with him. Hands down, the best day of my life, when I said yes to a lifetime with Aaron Ivey. I cannot imagine this life without him. I cannot imagine this journey of parenting without him. I cannot imagine ministry without him. He truly is my favorite person in the whole world.

We were still young, and still growing, and we'd still have many obstacles to work through, but we founded our union on equal love, trust, and dedication to each other. We believed in each other, pursued each other, cheered for each other, supported each other. Both of us loved the Lord and wanted to build our marriage in a way that glorified Him more than ourselves, and this remains our mission now with our marriage today.

Twenty years later, we're still doing these things.

Still complementing each other.

———

Your and my ideas of marriage are shaped by what we see or have seen in our lives. We're influenced by the married people around us.

When I was in the third grade, for example, I remember spending the night at my friend Ashley's house. Her parents' marriage was like a fairy tale to me. Her dad worked hard, and her mom kept the house well. I often saw her mom in a long, flowing satin robe at night. It was the most beautiful thing. I remember thinking I one day wanted to be married too, and wear a satin robe around the house.

As a college student, I watched my parents walk through a difficult season in their marriage. The tough patch they endured created ripple effects that impacted everyone in their circle, things that Satan still tries stirring up in my mind to place a sense of fear over my marriage. Yet I also watched God do a miracle in their relationship—the same kind of miracle I've seen Him do over and over in the lives of friends I've known throughout the past twenty years. What Satan sets out to destroy, God sets out to redeem and build up.

Both sets of my grandparents were married in the late 1940s, when men were going and coming from war, and women were raising babies and taking care of the home. As I became an adult, I began to see the struggles that marriages can endure at that age, when someone becomes distant or when someone becomes ill, as happened to both of my grandfathers.

You've had these same kinds of formative thoughts. Your own feelings. Your own observations. Your own take on how our culture views marriage today. All of it has rubbed off on you and factored into your thinking, becoming part of either your desire for marriage, your skepticism of marriage, or perhaps your decision to not want anything to do with marriage.

As for me, I have always desired marriage. I went to a private Christian college right out of high school, where there was a running joke that a lot of the girls only came to school to get their "MRS" degree. Maybe they were like me and just always saw themselves experiencing the kind of companionship that marriage could bring. Or maybe (also like me) they believed a man would fill some holes in their hearts for them.

I'll admit, I came into marriage thinking that Aaron would complete me, that my life would finally begin once we were married. I assumed my heart would never be hurt again. I thought he would fill the hole in my heart that yearned so badly to be unconditionally loved. I put a lot of pressure on him to never hurt me and never have arguments with me. I wanted a love that would always make me feel good and never make me uncomfortable.

Let's just say I brought a multi-piece set of baggage to our wedding day—baggage I wanted to keep a secret from him because I was certain he wouldn't want this kind of baggage in our house. And I'm guessing, so did you. Or, if you haven't married yet, you're well on your way to doing it. No matter where you're located today in your life journey, you too have ideas about what you expect from marriage. You don't need to be married to think these thoughts.

But though the world tells you a lot about marriage, and the church tells you a lot about marriage, we believe

God's Word is where we should all be getting our real perspectives on marriage. The Bible holds immense value for those of us yearning to love our husbands well in marriages that bless them, beautify us, and bring maximum glory to God.

Aaron and I think marriage has gotten a bad rap recently. Some people are disregarding the value of it. Others are using it to stifle a person's gifts and talents. Still others enter into it knowing that when the going gets tough, they'll run. There are just so many varying ideas around the gift of marriage. And if we're honest with you (which we always will be), we think even Christians haven't always done the best job of making marriage look like the true gift from God that it's meant to be. But for marriage to be what God had in mind, where it can stand up to real life and not back down from its amazing potential, we can't be buying into beliefs about marriage that clash with what God has always said about it.

I don't care who you are, something will come along to make your marriage difficult. Maybe this happened for you as early as your honeymoon (I'm serious), or maybe by Year Three. For us, it wasn't really until around Year Nine when circumstances conspired to make life hard at our house. In those moments, I knew there had to be more to marriage than just fun times and a constant companion. I needed a partner who was willing to walk through the fire with me. I needed a partner who was willing to keep the wind in my sails. I needed a partner who was willing to both lead *and* follow in different circumstances.

To complement me. Even as I complement him.

After being married for more than two decades now, I've learned marriage is so very beautiful. God created something for His children that magnifies Him in all sorts of ways. I've learned that great marriages don't happen overnight but are created through years of hard work and sacrifice on both spouses' parts.

I've also learned something else. Remember that desire of mine about Aaron *completing* me? How he would fill all the holes in my heart? That idea was never going to work out, I discovered. But I've grown to see that the way we *complement* each other does some wonderful things in both of our hearts. It's a beautiful picture of how God designed marriage to be.

———

I've been begging Aaron forever for us to renew our vows to each other one day. If I could have it my way, I'd love doing it on our twenty-fifth anniversary. We could go somewhere beautiful, preferably a beach. I'd get a lovely white dress; he'd look all handsome in skinny jeans and a white shirt; our kids would stand all around us; and we'd renew what we committed to one another all those years ago. It sounds downright dreamy to me.

Aaron always says no. Every time I ask. He doesn't think about it for even a single second. Automatic no. Because, he says, we made a covenant to each other when we said our vows the first time, and there is no reason ever to renew a covenant. Such a pastor statement! Don't you think? But I understand what he means. And I guess I secretly agree with him.

So I think I've changed my request to a vow *remembrance* ceremony. That's the party I really want!

We recently attended a party sort of like that—our friends Devin and Catherine's anniversary party. They invited their closest friends and family to celebrate the thirty years they'd been committed to each other in marriage. Their four kids were there; their new daughters-in-law were there. We stood outside their house on the back patio, and Aaron led them through a moment of remembering what God had done for them over the past three decades in their marriage.

I'll never forget what Devin said to his wife during that ceremony. As he held Catherine's hands, staring into her eyes while all of us watched, he said, "I recommit my life to you through the lens of experience." My eyes moistened with tears and I thought to myself, yes, *THAT* is what we do in marriage, day after day after day. We wake up each morning knowing exactly what yesterday held, and the day before that, and the day before that. And yet we commit to staying. We commit to love. We commit to serve. We commit to forgive. We commit to cheering. We commit to following.

We commit to each other because God has put us together, and because He thinks we're the best team, and because everything He really wants to accomplish in us will happen with *this* man and *this* woman, with *our* history, staying strong into *our* future.

———

Marriage is hard.

That may be the understatement of the year. We've experienced it ourselves and we've seen it in marriages all around us. But here's something else we believe.

Marriage is worth the fight.

Maybe you're young right now and don't have marriage on your brain at all; you're just wanting to prepare your heart for what might come. Or maybe you're early married and you want to keep building and repairing, making things better than they've ever been between you. Or maybe you're twenty-plus years in, like us, and you need a fresh kick in the pants to help you value the person that God put in your world to walk through life with you.

Wherever you're coming from, our prayer and hope is that you too can sense the deep honor of *complementing* your spouse in every area of your life. As we dive into these ten different ways that give you everyday, ongoing opportunities to complement your husband, I pray you will feel equal parts encouraged and challenged.

Growth in marriage is a good thing. We'll never arrive, of course. We'll be working on this relationship from now until the day we part through death. But we believe in you, and we believe in your marriage. And we believe God has given you and us, in His Word, the best way for all of us to live it out.

CHAPTER 1

Love

I have a thing for a good love story, and I'd bet you do as well. That's why Hollywood puts so much money and energy into making those stories come alive for us on the big screen. Each time we see a movie like that, we find ourselves rooting for love no matter what kind of journey it takes the characters on.

But most Hollywood love stories focus on the *feeling*, on the excitement and newness that new love brings. They know that something inside of us longs for that feeling of being loved just for who we are. We want the man to chase after us in the airport because he finally realizes he can't live without us. We want our husband to show up at work with two tickets to a weekend in Santa Fe, New Mexico, just because. We want sex on the beach and frolicking through the wildflowers while running hand in hand. The intense feelings associated with love are what we find ourselves desiring and idolizing.

The problem with this, of course, is that REAL LIFE doesn't always feel like NEW LOVE. Real life is hard. Real life requires more of us than sometimes our emotions can handle. I wish it was as easy as Julia Roberts says in *Nottinghill*: "I'm just a girl standing in front of a boy asking him to love her."

But it's not. Love takes way more work and is far more valuable than how they portray it in the movies.

What exactly is love anyway? The dictionary says love is both a noun and a verb. As a noun, love is an intense feeling of deep affection, as well as a great interest and pleasure in something. I agree with *Webster* on both of those definitions. As a verb, love means to feel a deep romantic or sexual attachment to someone. And I agree with all of that as well.

But what the dictionary *doesn't* tell you, which I want to add, is that love takes hard work to give.

Yes, loving your husband should be hard work.

Maybe you're thinking, *Whoa, Jamie, hold up. If love is hard work, then it's not love. Love should be easy. If it's true love, it shouldn't be hard.*

I'm sorry, have you been living on another planet? People are hard. People are mean. People drive us crazy. If you put two crazy, hard-to-love people together and then expect it to be easy . . .

Nope. Not at all.

Love is something we keep working on. Improving on. I'm much better at love today than ten years ago. Or, gosh, I sure hope so. For instance, Aaron loves words of affirmation, and I'm not the best at giving them. But over the years, I've worked hard at intentionally telling him how much I respect the work he does and how much it matters. And my work is paying off. I'm better at it now than I used to be. Still not a master of it, but I'm learning to love him better. Here's the thing though: it's taken me *hard work* to get here.

And that's okay. When you fall in love with your special someone, there's that intense initial feeling of deep affection. You have a great interest in him. You also feel sexual attraction. All those things are true, and fine, and good. But it's also true that as time moves on and as life happens, those intense feelings and sexual attractions begin to take hard work and time to create—hard work and time that you didn't have to put into it before.

Love is an action. Love is a choice. You choose to love over and over and over again. Day after day. Year after year.

And the challenge of it, surprisingly, is what makes it so beautiful.

———

When we think about love within marriage, we tend to go straight to the sexual intimacy that occurs between a husband and a wife. And just so you know, I'll definitely be going there with you in this book. I've saved up a whole chapter for it later on. But while sex is certainly one of the ways we show love to our husbands and they show it to us, it's not the ultimate way. There is so much more to love than just sex. You know that.

> Love is an action.
> Love is a choice.

But here's what I want you to think about that's not quite so obvious: *There is so much more to love than just love.*

I believe people in a lot of marriages are doing their best to love one another. But what I see so often today are women loving everyone around them better than they love their husbands. They *assume* they're loving him because they're married to him and doing stuff for him (like having sex with him and cooking his dinner). And yet their marriage is suffering because they're not sharing a genuine Christlike love for each other.

And true love, even married love, can only come from the example that Jesus Himself set for us.

Most people in the world, whether they claim to be a Christ-follower or not, would still claim that Jesus Christ was a good, moral man worth modeling our lives after. I certainly agree with that (though I think he's much more than *just* that). But we have a tendency to think that He's not our model for marriage because He was never married Himself. We could not be more wrong in holding to that opinion. We are meant to be imitators of Jesus in *all of our lives.* Marriage is no exception. Why *should* it be?

If you want to know how and why you can even begin to continually love this man you married, start with knowing that you can only love him because Jesus first loved you (1 John 4:19). Start by looking at the way God sent His Son for you and how Jesus died on a cross for you, and then you can start to comprehend the kind of love that you're meant to emulate in marriage.

Jesus' love for you was sacrificial. He didn't die for you because you're such a good person or because His Father made Him do it. No, Jesus died on a cross for you and your sins (and for me and my sins) because His love for us is so grand that He would do anything to restore us back to the Father.

Anything.

All right, so that's what Jesus' love is like. A sacrificial love. An *anything* love. That's the love He demonstrated toward us. And so with Jesus' brand of love as background, notice what He said *our* love is supposed to be like. The night before His arrest and crucifixion, He gave His disciples the following "new commandment."

> "A new commandment I give to you, that you love one another: just as I have loved you, you also are to love one another." (John 13:34)

"Just as I have loved you." That's the standard for how you and I are called to love our husbands. So if we truly want to be someone who looks more like Jesus every single day, here's our shot at it, right out of the gate every morning: to love our husbands the same way Jesus has loved us.

And tell me now, does that sound like *hard work* sometimes?

It is. And guess what? It gets even harder. The breakdown I see sometimes in relationships, especially in marriages, is that sacrificial love often seems so one-sided. It feels as though you're the one who's doing all the giving, all the loving, with zero guarantees that your husband will reciprocate that same love to you. It feels so risky. It's almost as if you're just setting yourself up to be hurt. And no one would wish that on themselves.

Yet if we truly want to be like Jesus—if we want our love for our husband to be *true love*—it must be Jesus' love, where we pour ourselves out completely for our man and then leave the results to God. I cannot guarantee that your husband will reciprocate the same type of love for you as you give to him, but I can guarantee you one thing: God will honor your love for your husband, just as He honored the faithful love of His Son for His people. Again, it may not result in being loved back faithfully by your husband. But if you ever expect to be, this is the way you do it.

By loving as Jesus loves.

So let's get really practical about this. The main verses that come to mind when we think of love—the verses that go into such beautiful, hard work detail about what Jesus' love is like—come from 1 Corinthians 13. You often hear them quoted at weddings, probably even at *your* wedding. Or they might be embroidered on a pillow you received as a gift from your great aunt. Maybe they're on a cool print that hangs in your bedroom, hallway, or office. My point here is that these words about love routinely come up when we talk about marriage, and though they weren't written with *marital* love immediately in mind, I think it's right to apply the wisdom they offer to marriage. If we want to be wives who love our husbands well—like Jesus loves us— here are the characteristics that should be found in us.

> God will honor your love for your husband, just as He honored the faithful love of His Son for His people.

- Love . . . is patient.
- Love . . . is kind.
- Love . . . is not envious.
- Love . . . is not boastful.

- Love . . . is not arrogant.
- Love . . . is not rude.
- Love . . . does not insist on its own way.
- Love . . . is not irritable.
- Love . . . is not resentful.
- Love . . . does not rejoice at wrongdoing.
- Love . . . rejoices with the truth.
- Love . . . bears all things.
- Love . . . believes all things.
- Love . . . hopes all things.
- Love . . . endures all things. (1 Cor. 13:4–8)

If we are to be women who love our husbands the way Christ loves us, we need to take these words to the core of our soul and beg God for the strength to be these things to our men. Will we get it right all the time? Absolutely not. I could write a story around each of these descriptions of love and tell you how I've failed to live them. We are selfish humans who, on our own, would only desire to make ourselves happy.

But love, as I said, is worth fighting for. It's worth sacrificing for. Jesus is our teacher in all things love, and His love toward us was sacrificial. Which means if we are to emulate Him and do all these things, we should expect it to be a sacrifice. Love is not flippant and easy; it is costly and difficult. That's what makes it so valuable.

Being kind when your husband doesn't deserve it feels unnatural. We like to treat people how they deserve. And yet, praise God, that's now how He looks at us, am I right? "He has not dealt with us as our sins deserve" (Ps. 103:10 CSB). He doesn't give us what's coming to us. He gives us His love.

———

I do love Aaron so much. It's true. But my love for him feels different today than it did twenty years ago. Different is not always bad; it's just different. The love I had for him on our wedding day was so very real, but it was all the love I could muster at that time. And I guess it was all I needed. Our life was easy. It was full of bliss. We were young and in love.

But when I think about loving Aaron now, I see a much bigger picture of what love looks like. I see a love that remains even when we're in a fight. I feel a love for him that amazingly is still capable of growing stronger, like when he reassures me for the four millionth time that I am indeed a good mom. I'm still surprised at how much love overflows from my heart for him when we're walking through a stressful season and we take time out for a date night. I love him a million times more today than I did on our wedding day. And the only way this happens is because I have chosen every single day to love him more than I did the day before.

I want to love him like Jesus loves me.

When we walked through our hardest season of parenting so far, and then our first hard season of marriage, I had to make a daily choice to choose love—to choose to give love and receive love even when it would have been much easier to shut down and be closed off. Because as much as I love the idea of love being a passive verb that is easily attainable, I know it takes choosing. For all of us. It takes kindness when we want deep in our hearts to tear our husband down. It takes throwing away the scorecard when we desperately want to add up points against him. It takes forgiving when we would feel better keeping a death grip on his wrongdoings. It takes grace when all we want to give is punishment.

It takes all of these things day after day. And what I've found to be true in my own life is that I love loving Aaron, and I have a strong suspicion that he too loves loving me.

CHAPTER 2

Serve

Early in our marriage, I set out to win the "Best Wife in the World" award. I was certain if such an award existed, I would not only be a top finalist, I would take home the gold for sure. I would be the kind of wife that other women would dream about being. I would be the kind of wife who would make any husband happy. I would model what a perfect wife looked like.

A few years into this game of trying to win the award, I conceded to the fact that the award was indeed fake. I had been its sole originator, judge, presenter, and smiling recipient. For years I thought to myself, *You will not find a better wife on the planet*, and I made it my mission to keep living up to this self-proclaimed standard year after year.

There were many problems, however, with what I was doing, as I'm sure you can figure out on your own. On the plus side, I WAS A REALLY GOOD WIFE. Couldn't argue that. But on the negative side, I was forcing myself to keep winning this make-believe award every single year. Or else. *Or else what?* you might ask.

Or else Aaron would leave me.

That was the kicker. I needed to be the best so that he would have no reason to look outside the home for a new woman. I know it may sound crazy to you, and I can admit I too now find it crazy, but to me, at the time, it was as real as real can be. It was the best motivator I could think of to make sure Aaron and I didn't become a statistic of infidelity in our marriage. Because that was my biggest fear in life: the fear that my husband would wake up one day and decide he wanted a new wife. A new sex partner. A new best friend. A new woman to chase God with. It plagued me so much that I started living the kind of life I thought would *guarantee* it would never happen. I would serve Aaron in whatever way he wanted serving so that he would have no cause for leaving me.

He wanted a guy's night out? And I was exhausted from solo-parenting all day? No problem. He liked the bedroom to look a certain way? No problem. He had a plan for something he wanted to spend money on and what he wanted us to be saving for? No problem. I did whatever it took to make him happy.

As you can imagine, this was draining to me, and the worst part is that it was fake to Aaron. From the outside—even most of the time from the inside—I did look like the perfect wife. But at what cost? I was serving my man for the primary purpose of keeping him from leaving me. It was sick, and it was suffocating me.

> That was my biggest fear in life: the fear that my husband would wake up one day and decide he wanted a new wife.

I'll never forget a conversation one day with my friend Tiffany. She knew about my fear of Aaron leaving me, and I suspect she saw me working really hard to make sure he didn't have a legit reason for cheating on me. She looked me straight in the eye that day and said, "You know, Jamie, you can't keep Aaron from making those choices." I was floored by that. Tiffany was obviously not as good of a wife as I was, or she'd have known better than to say stuff like that. Or was she?

These words of hers echoed in my brain and heart for months, until finally God broke me. I started to see the way I'd been living, loving, and serving my husband had actually become detrimental to our marriage. I was giving Aaron so much of me, but it was all built on fear, not love. My reason for striving after this "Wife of the Year" award (which, again, is fake and does not exist) was all to protect my heart. It had nothing to do with him, with his heart, or even with our marriage for that fact. My desire to serve Aaron was self-protective. It didn't come from an overflow of my love for God.

A shift happened in me around that time, and I'm so thankful for it because God revealed something about His character to me that has actually propelled me into loving Aaron much better than I'd ever loved him before.

It all comes down to what it truly means to be a *servant.*

You see, there can be a big difference of opinion about the definition of that word. And no matter where you find yourself right now in your attitude toward servanthood, I can promise you God has a better picture of what it looks like to be a servant than what we've seen, imagined, or have been portraying.

As with everything else in our lives, Jesus is the ultimate example of servanthood. Can you think of a greater servant than Jesus? I dare you.

- Jesus served His disciples the night before He was to be crucified.
- Jesus served guests at a wedding one day by turning water into wine.
- Jesus served Lazarus and his family by raising him from the dead.
- Jesus served people fish and loaves when there was nothing else to give.

Jesus served and served and served, even though all along He was *GOD*. That's because "even the Son of Man," He said, "came not to be served but to serve, and to give his life as a ransom for many" (Mark 10:45). The One who receives our praise laid down His life for us. The One who sustains our breath gave His own away. The One who breathed life into man died for all of mankind.

Paul wrote a message about Jesus' example of servanthood that I think needs to be at the forefront of our minds when we think about our marriages:

> Do nothing from selfish ambition or conceit, but in humility count others more significant than yourselves. Let each of you look not only at his own interests, but also to the interests of others.
>
> Have this mind among yourselves, which is yours in Christ Jesus, who, though he was in the form of God, did not count equality with God a thing to be grasped, but emptied himself, by taking the form of a servant, being born in the likeness of men. And being found in human form, he humbled himself by becoming obedient to the point of death, even death on a cross. (Phil. 2:3–8)

We think this is all really good teaching in terms of how we should treat other people. But how we should treat our husbands? I mean, after a wedding ceremony, after a few kids, and after several years of life, we think these commands couldn't possibly apply to our marriage, could they? We teach them to our children, we expect them from our coworkers. Yet when it comes to the marriage relationship, no thanks. We're out of the servanthood business.

But when I shifted my focus from serving Aaron so that he would never leave me, to serving Aaron because of how much God loved me, everything changed for me in our marriage. I wonder if you might see the same outcome.

———

Becoming a servant brings zero glory to a person. It's true. Think about it for a second: to become a servant means to give yourself to someone else. For *their* sake. In the make-believe life I told you about, I was being a good servant, but I was doing it to *receive* something. For myself. It gave me a false sense of security.

I can say with confidence today that I serve my husband well in our marriage. But it's not because of what's in it for me anymore. It's because of how much God loves me. Does my fear about Aaron leaving me still pop up in my heart every once in a while? Yes, but not for one second anymore do I believe I can serve him enough to keep him happy and in love with me. That's too much pressure on both of us.

I want to be an emulator of Jesus—period! Therefore, I want to be a woman who serves her husband well.

Now I get it if this idea of being your husband's *servant* strikes you the wrong way. Even my own defenses go up when I hear a sermon about wives serving their husbands. I find myself thinking, "What's the final point of this sermon, because I need to know if I can trust you. I need to know if you value me, or if you're telling me to be a doormat with no mind of her own." Here's what I'm really asking in those moments: "Are you saying the same things to the men in the room as you're saying to me?"

Servanthood within a marriage is not designated for wives only. It's not that only wives serve and only husbands lead. Absolutely not. Both partners should live with a servanthood attitude that seeks to serve each other as an overflow of our hearts. We don't do it to earn the other's love or to fit a cultural norm. We do it because our love for God moves us toward serving everyone around us. And I said *everyone* for a reason. We can't forget that we are all called—every single one of us—to "serve one another through love" (Gal. 5:13 csb). God calls every single one of His people to serve, well, every single one of His people. Yes, there's a "servant class" in the kingdom of God—and every single citizen is in that class! Serving each other is an equal opportunity command! So it makes sense that serving "one another" includes our husbands—more than that, I think it should *start with* our husbands.

Again, I realize how this clashes with what we naturally want. We tend to be a transactional society. We often think, *What will I get if I do something for you? What will you do for me in return?* We keep track, we keep score, and we refuse to go above and beyond unless we're reasonably assured of getting a return on our investment.

But I'd like to present a different way of seeing your marriage. What if you both tried to "outserve" each other, to see which one could serve the other more? I like contests, as you can tell, and I think this is a good one. Except there's no scorekeeping. It's purely an overflow of your heart. You serve because you love. You serve because you've been loved and been served so deeply by the Father. There's no expectation, no penalties, no scorekeeping, and both of you just give and give and give.

That's a sure-fire win in my book.

———

I grew up seeing both of my grandmothers serve their husbands quite well. And I figured the ways I saw them serving were just how wives were supposed to do it. In my twenty-five years of knowing both my grandfathers, I never once saw them do a single thing in the kitchen. I realize I didn't live every day with either one of them, but I feel as though I have a good handle on how the duties were delegated in their home. Wives were to cook, clean, and take care of the kids; husbands were to work, make the money, and take care of the bills.

By no means am I saying that any of these things they did were wrong, but I do want to make sure we aren't equating servanthood toward our husbands as *only* those things. In my home, for instance, Aaron does most of the cooking. Does that make me a bad wife? Not at all. In my home we both work and earn income for the family. Does that make me a bad wife? Not at all. Servanthood is a posture of the heart that translates into the actions we do.

When we read a book on servanthood written toward women, often it goes this way: do whatever needs to be done in order to make your man happy. Cook for him, wash his clothes, look pretty, and make the children behave. I actually agree with a lot of that, but society has taken it and twisted it in so many ways that it actually feels dirty when I read those words.

What if we truly looked at servanthood in marriage as a dance: a two-person act of laying down our lives for one another. *Complementing* one another. Sometimes more of him; sometimes more of me; but always both of *us*. What if, as women yearning to love our husbands well, we began to view our relationship through the eyes of the gospel, the gospel that says God so loved the world that He sent His only Son for us? The gospel says servanthood and love go hand and hand. *Hand in hand.* That makes for the best dancing anyway.

———

I've figured out one of the best ways to serve my husband, and though it sounds downright unconventional, it works for us. Aaron is a creative. Like, a legit creative. This means he works with his mind, with a lot of competing ideas, and sometimes his mind gets a little overwhelmed and needs a break, needs to breathe some fresh air. He needs to be alone with himself and his thoughts, to regroup, to recharge. I *get* that about him.

So, watch this. We had been married for about ten years when Aaron asked one day if he could go away for a weekend. *Alone*—as in, I wasn't invited, nor were the kids. Now at this point in our marriage, I was a stay-at-home mama, which meant the day-to-day kids' stuff was primarily my responsibility. Which meant when he asked for a trip away—alone—I'll admit my defenses were a little high. I'm sure I thought things like, *Oh, sure, you really NEED a break.* Or, *Must be nice to take a relaxing, seven-hour drive and have peace and quiet for three whole days.* Did I ever say any of those things out loud? To him or to anyone else?

The only thing that matters is that I said yes. Because even if deep down I did think some of those thoughts, I love my husband. I truly want what's best for him. And what I've discovered over the years is that Aaron truly does need that time, and when he gets it, he is not only a better creative but he's a better husband and father as well. The end game is monumental in our marriage and in our family.

So one of the ways that I have served my husband best over the past decade of our marriage is by letting him head out on the open roads to west Texas once in a while with my full blessing where he can breathe a little. It's usually three or four days. And although there have been seasons when the timing has felt bad and it wasn't the easiest on me to solo-parent for those days, the sacrifice on my part has always been worth it.

Aaron has said to me more times than I can count how thankful he is for my sacrifice in this area of his life. There's no doubt he understands the weight of what it requires on me for him to get away. I'll admit the sacrifice was a lot larger when our kids were younger, when life was more chaotic at home and most of my waking hours were spent parenting. It's still a sacrifice today, but in a different, less intense way.

And the dance goes both ways. There are times when, laying down my "perfect wife" award and instead deciding to be human and vulnerable and honest, I tell Aaron I need a break (or some backup) too. And he serves me back. He'll give me the time I need to travel for work or a weekend away with some girlfriends to catch my breath. We do the dance. We serve "one another."

What about you? The way you serve your husband might look nothing like the example I described earlier.

But whatever it may be, I encourage you to find it, dig into it, and see how you can sacrificially serve your man.

Servanthood is hardly glorified in our society, but it is always glorified in the eyes of God. Serving those around us is what people who follow Jesus do. Everywhere. With everyone. But I pray it would start happening more consistently in our marriages so that we would imitate the servanthood of Jesus in our homes—sacrificial giving with no expectation. And no fake awards.

CHAPTER 3

Cheer

I'm not sure if the saying "opposites attract" is true or not, but Aaron and I are so very different, and yet so very attracted to each other.

Aaron, for example, has written hundreds of songs in his four decades of life. I suspect he'll write hundreds more in his next four decades. I, on the other hand, have written exactly zero songs in my four decades, and I suspect the same will be said about the next four.

But the contrast in our musical abilities is hardly the only one of our differences. Here's another: I love Saturdays in the fall because I can watch endless hours of college football. (Hook 'em Horns!) Yet I cannot think of one complete game of college football that Aaron has ever watched.

Here's another: He loves to spend hours in the kitchen creating elaborate, delicious meals for our family. In fact, I get nervous when Aaron is out of town for the weekend, not because I'm worried about an intruder, but because it means I'll be responsible for feeding all these kids of ours while he's gone.

And still another: My idea of a perfect day involves hours upon hours lying in the sun by the beach, listening to the waves with a good book in my hand. His idea of a perfect day involves no sun and lots of quiet.

> You will not find anyone cheering louder for my man than me.

We are so very different. We always have been.

Yet, check again at the top of this chapter and make note of the title: "Cheer." You'll see I'm not writing this chapter on the theme of *differences*. I'm using our differences to make a point about *cheerleading*, how despite the many ways in which Aaron and I are dissimilar, you will not find anyone cheering louder for my man than me.

To explain further, let's do a deep-dive on this music thing.

I don't understand for a second what makes one song better than another. I mean, I'll stop everything I'm doing and sing along to "I Will Always Love You," no matter if it's Whitney or Dolly singing it. I'll throw my hands in the air like I just don't care when Montel Jordan tells me to do it. Worship music is my jam, and there aren't many ways I feel more connected to God than when I'm belting out songs to Him and about Him. I love to sing, but I am also confident in the knowledge that I *cannot* sing. Don't worry, that's not a low blow to myself. It's just a fact. And I can handle it. I'm better at other things. Singing is never going to make my list of talents.

My point in saying all this is that even if I don't have a clue what it means to be a songwriter, or to produce music, or to lead people in worship, I will cheer and cheer for my man—who *can* do all those things—for as long as he's alive. We made the conscious decision a long time ago that we would be each other's loudest cheerleaders in life. And I would go out on a limb to say: this one decision has impacted our marriage in perhaps more profound ways than any other. Being absolutely sure that no matter what happens to me in life, I have this one man in my corner, cheering for me—it alters the way I live. When challenges come, I know I'm not alone. When I feel defeated, I know he is for me. When I am at the end, he is there to help me keep moving.

He's my biggest cheerleader. And I am his.

No matter how many great songs Aaron writes, or how many thousands of people he leads in worship, I have decided that I will cheer him on. When Aaron writes a new song and he wants to share it with me, I consciously stop what I'm doing and listen. I don't hear melodies, and I don't know the difference between a bridge and a chorus, but I am 100 percent in the moment with him, listening. I give him honest feedback—and tell him that I love it!

There have indeed been moments when I've failed at this. Believe it or not, I'm not just sitting around all day waiting for Aaron to bring me his latest song to share with me. I'm living my life over here—working in my office, taking care of things in the home, driving kids around. You get the point. But the times when Aaron has come to me and asked me to listen to a song of his, and I *didn't* give him the time of day—those have been the times when I've failed him. Failed to be a cheerleader in the moment. Failed to give him something that truly only I can give him.

Here's the truth when it comes to Aaron's music. I am not his litmus test about the song itself. Remember, I don't understand the mechanics of harmony and melody. I don't have a handle on the finer points of song construction. I don't know what key it's in or anything about its tempo markings. But what my man wants from me is not a music critique. He just needs a listening ear and an encouraging word. He wants his woman to cheer him on.

That I can do. I can cheer, even if I don't fully understand.

———

Private cheering is highly valuable within our marriage, as I would suspect is true in most marriages (though many of us may need to work on this!), but *public cheering* is a whole other level of encouragement that we can give each other. I don't know one person who doesn't love to be publicly praised. Even if you're a self-proclaimed introvert who says you hate having attention thrown your way, I would guess you don't mind someone praising you in front of people every once in a while. It feels good. It makes you feel noticed and appreciated.

If Aaron never publicly proclaimed his love for me, it would not feel real to me. And if I never proclaimed my encouragement to him in front of others, I'm guessing he would find it somewhere else.

Some of the most uncomfortable moments for me are when someone is putting someone down in front of others, especially when that someone is their spouse! Surely you know what I'm talking about. I've seen this dynamic play out over and over and over again, and it always seems to go something like this: They get that critical look in their eye and in their tone of voice. More than likely they're trying to be funny, hoping for a good laugh at the expense of this person they married, although sometimes what they say is downright spiteful and mean. No matter, it is so extremely uncomfortable for everyone there.

There have been plenty of times when I've screwed up with this myself. Again, usually in trying to get a laugh from people, I've made my husband the butt of a joke. But in most cases, as soon as the punch line exits my mouth and I'm waiting for everyone's reaction, I can see by the look on Aaron's face that my joke was indeed not funny to him, that while I was trying to lighten the mood or make people laugh, it cost him something. I'd momentarily cared more about myself than him.

Thankfully this is not my norm, but I've had to learn this lesson throughout our marriage. Complementing each other through mutual respect and encouragement—especially in a day when anyone can publicly criticize anyone—is a beautiful thing to experience in marriage. To know that my husband would never intentionally put me down in other people's presence gives me confidence. It makes our union stronger. I think we owe that to each other.

———

> Let no corrupting talk come out of your mouths, but only such as is good for building up, as fits the occasion, that it may give grace to those who hear. (Eph. 4:29)

Do you remember the saying you heard when you were a kid: "Sticks and stones may break my bones, but words will never hurt me"? I get the reasoning behind why we teach our kids this cute little saying, in hopes they'll let mean words roll off their back like water off a duck. Except the fact is that words actually really do hurt. They sting badly. I can recount specific words that have been said to me, or about me, that hurt way worse than when I broke my arm in fifth grade.

I mean, that broken arm really bugged me for a while. I had to wear a plastic bag over my cast all during summer vacation pool parties. It was so hot at Disneyland that I thought I was going to burn up. But it has long since healed. I have no residual pain in that arm. Honestly, I'd have to think super hard to even remember exactly which arm I broke.

But words—oh, their sting can last a long time. Some of the stings last all of our days on the earth. It pains me to think that my mouth could ever spew the kind of hateful, hurtful, corrupting words toward anyone that would stick with them forever. I'd especially hate to think I'd do that to my husband.

And yet, I know that I have. I know that my words have gotten the best of me at times and I have made mistakes in what I've said. In those moments when I've done that to Aaron, or he's done it to me, we fall back on sort of an unspoken pact between us that says no matter how innocent we thought our words to be, or what we actually meant by them, if they were hurtful, we will own them and apologize. Pronto.

Is that always easy? Of course not. But do I cherish my husband more than I cherish being right or understood? Of course.

Cheering for those around us means that we use our words to bring them up and not bring them down. Complementing each other in our marriage looks the same way: both people yearning to speak life into each other, yearning to be the one who builds up and doesn't tear down. I want to be a builder of Aaron's life, not a destroyer. A cheerleader.

———

A few years ago, I was flying home from Nashville after some meetings and was standing at a table next to the gate where I was waiting for my flight. It was one of those high tables that had room for more than just one person to use it, so while I was minding my own business, working on my computer there, a man nonchalantly came up and stood across from me. Now what you need to know about me is that when I travel, I have zero desire to talk to anyone. (If you ever see me in an airport and I look like "don't talk to me," you'll know it's nothing personal.) Obviously, as a Christian, I know I should be looking for opportunities to tell everyone around me about Jesus, but really, I just want to be left alone when traveling. Hate me if you will.

This man, though, apparently didn't get my body language and started a conversation. We ended up talking the entire thirty minutes until we both left to board our planes. He was kind. He was younger than me. And he seemed genuinely interested in what I was doing in Nashville. If you're waiting for the scandal here, there isn't one. There was no harm, no foul, and we eventually went our separate ways.

But until the day I die, I will never forget what I felt like as I walked toward my plane. My *first* thought was how this man had made me feel important, special, interesting. My *second* thought was that I wanted to throw up because of those feelings. So as I waited to board the plane, I called my friend Amanda[1] and told her about *both* of these feelings before catching my plane for home.

---

[1] Find friends you can immediately call when you screw up. It's the best feeling.

This scenario is not an example of why men and women can't be friends,[2] nor is it a declaration that men and women can't have random conversations at an airport. What this story does for me is remind me how much I need to hear those things from Aaron and how much he needs to hear them from me. Otherwise, they feel too good coming from other people.

I can't recall what our marriage was like that day, whether we were in a good place or a bristly place. I can't recall if there was anything stressful going on with our kids or what other challenges we might have had at home at the time. All I recall is feeling super cheered on by a stranger at an airport, and my husband was nowhere to be seen. It's a feeling I enjoyed and immediately hated. Do you hear me?

I often recall this story when our lives are going so fast that I forget to encourage or cheer Aaron on in what he's doing. We have a tendency to put our heads down and just do our day-to-day jobs, whether we're going to the office, creating music, or trying to keep our kids alive. It's so easy to forget to look around and be an encourager to our husbands.

---

[2] Remember the movie *When Harry Met Sally*.

I don't want anyone cheering louder for my man than me. No matter what craziness our home may be experiencing, I want my encouraging voice to rise higher than all the other noise. And Aaron would say the same in reverse.

Makes me want to . . . *cheer*!

CHAPTER 4

Lead

It's always a surprise to people when they find out that Aaron and I never discussed adoption—not once—before we were married. The surprise is because three of our four children joined our family through adoption. You'd think a couple who adopted *THREE TIMES* must have gone into their marriage planning for it.[3] Except that's not the case for us at all. We had exactly zero conversations about adoption prior to saying "I do" or even in the two years that followed. God simply moved through the people in our community and the church we were attending to open up our eyes and hearts to it.

---

[3] Or that they have fertility issues, which I know you're wondering, so I'll answer your question: We have no idea if we had fertility issues or not. God kept moving our hearts toward adoption.

Adoption was new to us, different, a part of our family planning that we could never have imagined. I gave birth to our first son two and a half years after we were married, and that same year we walked into an adoption agency and told them we were willing to help out however they needed. This led us to welcoming our second son, who was born in Texas, while we still lived in Tennessee.

We were the cutest little family of four, and Aaron was quite happy. Two boys, mom + dad, the "perfect" combo. I, on the other hand, couldn't shake the feeling that I wasn't done as a mom. I can't explain it except to say: if you've felt it, you know what I mean. I was happy; I loved my kids; it wasn't a discontentment issue. It was truly just a feeling I couldn't shake that we needed to add more kids to our family.

I would occasionally broach the subject with Aaron, and he was 100 percent sure that we were done, that our family was complete. I would then tell him what I told you: I couldn't shake the feeling that there were more kids for us. And he would tell me he knew that we were indeed so very done, that *he* couldn't shake the feeling that there were *no* more kids for us. We were at a standstill for sure.

It was a roadblock. More than a roadblock, it was a disaster zone most days. Not only could I not understand Aaron, I believed he was wrong and that I was right. Our discussions turned into arguments, and I was left feeling as though we were not only on two different teams but were playing two different games. He wasn't getting me, and I wasn't getting him. We were at a loss, both of us thinking we were right, and both of us wanting to lead the way. I wanted to lead so badly in this area. And by leading, I mean I wanted Aaron to do exactly what I wanted him to do and what I thought was best for our family.

Enter wisdom. I decided to try a tactic that a wise woman suggested to me. She encouraged me to drop it—stop nagging him, stop trying to convince him—and invest my energies instead into praying for God to change one or the other of our hearts.

So that's what I did. I dropped it. My leadership in the adoption decision turned into prayer.

I admit this may not sound like the greatest leadership skill or strategy in the world, but I'm now convinced more than ever that great leaders pray as they lead. Great leaders in any area of life—whether it be in marriage or in a small business or in church as a pastor—make prayer their first play on offense when they're wanting to lead out on something.

I began to pray the boldest prayer I've yet to pray. It was bold because I was laying down my ability to change Aaron. I was laying down my wants and needs and truly asking God to show up and unite us. I prayed, "God bring us together. Change his heart or change mine. But please, Lord, make us unified."

Great leaders pray as they lead.

I prayed and shut my mouth, and let God do what God does best.

Without sounding like I'm boasting here, I need you to know something. I didn't flippantly ask him to change one of our hearts while I was crossing my fingers behind my back, hoping to trick God into changing only Aaron's heart. For myself, yes, I was convinced my motherhood wasn't complete, BUT . . . I was 100 percent willing to lay it down if God said otherwise. I meant it. I wasn't playing around. I offered up my own heart to be changed too. And if so, we'd stick with what we had.

Prayer worked.

God showed up.

Not at first. Not even days later. For months I shut my mouth and prayed this prayer. (Little sidebar here: one good thing that came out of those months was that Aaron and I stopped arguing over the issue, and my prayer life became consistently on point.) But the greatest thing was that God moved in our marriage and changed hearts. Half a year later while sitting on a swing outside of Camp Tejas in Giddings, Texas, Aaron looked at me and said the words I had hoped he'd say but was prepared to never hear: "I'm ready to add to our family through adoption."

Now you would've thought, as soon as Aaron finished saying those words, I was on speed dial with an adoption agency, but I wasn't. I had seen God do something miraculous in us, and I was willing to wait on Him to lead us into the next steps. We finished our summer travels[4] and headed back home. It was there that I began to research and begin our adoption process.

One night while Aaron was away playing music, I was reading a blog I'd begun following after taking a trip

---

[4] Aaron was in a band, Spur58, and they travelled and led worship at youth and college events. In the summer he was gone for about ten weeks in a row, and thankfully the kids and I were able to join him for a few every year.

the previous year to Haiti. Real Hope for Haiti[5] is a children's rescue center that helps malnourished children and then works to reunite them with their families. On this particular night their blog had listed three children in need of a family, and I kid you not: from the moment my eyes locked onto this one child, I knew he was our son. I can't explain it, and I know it sounds weird. I'd viewed hundreds of profiles in the past few weeks about children who needed families, but none had stood out to me. *This child did.*

Aaron arrived home and I told him the news. I had found our son. To say he was apprehensive is an understatement. Once again, we began the traditional dance of the Iveys: Aaron, slow and thoughtful, methodically working through his worries, fears, and uncertainties; and me, full of confidence, and LET'S DO THIS! It was awkward. We were both so scared in our own ways. I went back into prayer. It had worked before.

Just to spoil the lead here, the photo I had seen was of our son Amos, and we've now been a family for more

---

[5] They do beautiful work and I've been honored to spend many nights with them while we were in the adoption process. See https://realhopeforhaiti.org/.

than a decade. That night of seeing his picture on a website led us down a grueling, two-and-a-half-year journey to bring him home to us.

I could list a handful of other times when I've led out on things in our marriage and Aaron has followed. It's never a contest to see who takes the lead; it's a listening to the Holy Spirit in both of our lives. There's no unspoken rule in our home about who gets to make the final call on our life choices, yet there is a built-in trust now over years of mutual following, and mutual leading, in ways that always glorify God and never diminish the other person. We trust each other. And more than that, we trust God to lead us both well.

———

I did a quick Amazon search for books that had the word "leadership" in the title, and not to my surprise, I found more than sixty thousand titles to choose from. Everyone is longing to be a good leader. Leadership can look different at different times and seasons in your life. Some days you may be leading people at work; at other times you may be leading your children. On other days your leading may feel small in comparison to others, though it is leading just the same.

But let's stop beating around the bush. I want to talk now about what everyone is wondering here. *Who is the true leader in the home?* Is it the husband or is it the wife? Another quick Amazon search for "leadership in marriage" pulled up over five hundred results. And after a quick scan, I noticed a lot of them were screaming either (1) MEN RUN THE SHOW or (2) NO ONE TELLS A WOMAN WHAT TO DO.[6]

Maybe we should skip the books and go right to the main Book. Paul writes in Ephesians:

> Wives, submit to your own husbands, as to the Lord. For the husband is the head of the wife even as Christ is the head of the church, his body, and is himself its Savior. Now as the church submits to Christ, so also wives should submit in everything to their husbands. (Eph. 5:22–24)

---

[6] Not all of them. I'm being dramatic, but this is the reality of what we think the options are in marriage.

This particular verse has been used for so much evil in the world. Men have used this verse to demand submission from their wives. Pastors have used this verse with their congregations to demand it of married women. I admit sometimes this verse sounds cruel to women and hard to truly understand. *Why do I have to be the one to submit? It doesn't seem fair to have someone OVER me.*

Yet what we see in these verses is actually a surprisingly beautiful picture of Jesus and His bride, the church. If we can loosen our fear of the word "submit" for a second and view this passage as a moving illustration of what Jesus has done for us, we might just see what we've been missing about the responsibilities of both husbands and wives in the home.

We tend to get stuck on that second word of verse 22—"submit"—and miss what's coming up in verse 25, where Paul adds, "Husbands, love your wives, as Christ loved the church and gave himself up for her." Tim Keller makes this comment:

> As we shall see, each of these exhortations has a distinct shape—they are not identical tasks. And yet each partner is called to sacrifice for the other

> in far-reaching ways. Whether we are husband or wife, we are not to live for ourselves but for the other. And that is the hardest yet single most important function of being a husband or wife in marriage.[7]

See, *neither* of these—wives submitting or husbands loving—leaves room for anyone to be domineering in marriage.

In the verses leading up to the "submit" word in Ephesians 5, Paul is telling all of us what it looks like to be filled with the Holy Spirit, to be walking in the Spirit. We're to be marked by joy and gladness, by gratitude and worship, and by "*submitting to one another out of reverence for Christ*" (Eph. 5:21, italics mine). Submission is what ALL of us do in the church—submitting first to Christ, and then because of our love for Him, submitting to others. We treat everyone else in the manner we've already read about in Philippians: "in humility count others more significant than yourselves" (Phil. 2:3).

---

[7] Tim and Kathy Keller, *The Meaning of Marriage* (New York: Penguin, 2011), 50.

We're going to flesh out this idea of submission more in the next chapter, and hopefully you will see how even in submission to God and to each other we see the surprising beauty in marriage.

The problem is, we often confuse the *actions* of leading and following with the *postures* of submission and sacrificial love that Paul describes in Ephesians 5. It's true that the Bible gives husbands and wives different postures in marriage, but that does not mean husbands *always* lead and wives *always* follow.

In fact, the ultimate leader in our home is neither Aaron nor me—it's Jesus Christ. Both of us submit to Him and follow His will. He is our leader, and we'll follow Him wherever He goes. Part of following Him means that Aaron sacrificially loves me the way Jesus loves the church, and I submit to his sacrificial love the way the church submits to the love of Christ. Within those God-given postures toward one another, sometimes one of us leads, and sometimes the other leads. But whichever one of us is leading at any particular moment, Jesus is *always* our leader.

So as we lead and follow in our marriages, may we lead like Jesus led, follow like Jesus followed, serve like Jesus served, and lay down our own wants and desires like Jesus did.

CHAPTER 5

Follow

Where you go I will go" (Ruth 1:16).

The first person accredited with saying these words is Ruth in the Old Testament, but they have now become a highlight of so many weddings I've attended. I get butterflies in my stomach every time I hear them spoken. Twenty years married, and I would still say easily to Aaron, "Where you go, I'll go" But I'd also need to add, "and so will these four kids and two dogs!" Following someone is a high honor which none of us should take lightly.

Following your husband in marriage is and should be a beautiful act of complementing him. It is and should look like a beautiful picture of love and trust, all rolled up into one. I'm fully aware as you're reading this chapter that you could be a bit tense because you don't know where I'm going to take this. (I hope I eased your fears a bit in the last chapter.) Can I admit that the word "follow" in marriage has at times made me feel a bit tense as well?

Two avenues of "following" are often taught in reference to marriage. The first is that of a woman who has no brain, doesn't think for herself, would jump off a cliff if her husband told her to do it, and doesn't get a voice in anything. She aimlessly and methodically follows her husband in whatever he says their family should do. The second is that of a woman who claims, "I don't follow anyone but myself," who storms around demanding to be in charge or she's out. This woman refuses to follow her husband because . . . well, she doesn't follow anyone!

Both are extremes. I'm fully aware of that. But both have actually come to my mind in preparing to write this chapter on *following*, and I think they've probably entered your mind in the few minutes we've been thinking about it together.

But I'd like to propose a better way to talk about following. This entire idea of complementing your husband in marriage is not only biblical but is intended for our flourishing in marriage. It is intended to give us a small glimpse into how Jesus loves *His* bride, the church.

Everything in marriage is about complementing each other, and therefore so is the idea of following.

But there's a negative connotation attached to being a follower. We tell our kids, "Be a leader, not a follower." We tell ourselves to be in charge and make people want to follow us. We tend to believe that leaders are the ones who matter, and followers must be weak and voiceless. But the truth is, this world is made up of both leaders *and* followers. We need both to make the world go around.

As I look at my four children, I see some who have incredible leadership qualities, and I see some that I hope will have incredible following skills because they're not naturally gifted as leaders. My prayer for them is that they will find a great leader to follow, because not everyone can be the leader at all times in life.

But when I think about my marriage, there is only one ultimate leader in this home, as I said, and His name is Jesus Christ. Aaron and I both follow Him with everything that is in us. Between the two of us, though, we complement ourselves as both leader *and* follower, depending on the need of the moment and the places where we've shown capabilities, understanding, and wisdom. The whole thing is based on our submission to Christ and our trust, love, and admiration for each other.

When we were about to send our first child off to kindergarten, I struggled more than I ever imagined with sending him to public school. This struggle seemed to arise out of nowhere because I myself was a public school girl. I'm a fan of the public school system. I didn't feel called to homeschool my kids, and quite frankly there wasn't an extra penny in our budget for private school fees. None of my worrying made sense. And yet I was scared to send *MY BABY* off to where I was certain the devils of the world would attack him, and where with all his five-year-old strength he would turn his back on the one true God.[8]

As Aaron and I would discuss (a.k.a. argue) about the idea of public school for our sweet, innocent five-year-old, he assured me that we were doing the right thing, that we were making the right decision, that we couldn't be dominated by fear but needed to trust our kids into the Lord's care—that our son was more *God's* child than he was actually ours.

---

[8] You guys, it's true I am quite dramatic, and yet I must tell you these are not exaggerated thoughts—I really thought them!

Still, I was a wreck about it. But I began to remember a prayer I had prayed before, and I asked God to unify our hearts on this subject. I began to pray more about it; I began to listen to Aaron more about it; I began to trust God with my child more.

I'll never forget the day my heart changed. I was out for a run, and this particular running path took me right in front of the school that my son was set to attend in the fall. I had run by this school hundreds of times, but on this particular day I stopped and prayed this same prayer I had been praying, asking God to unite Aaron and me on this decision, and for me to trust God with my son no matter what we decided. I stopped running, stared at the school . . . and tears began just pouring out of my eyes. God moved in my heart in that moment, and I'll never forget that feeling. I trusted God in that moment.

But I also trusted my husband in that moment. I was ready now to follow his leadership in this decision.

———

I decided in 1999, when I became a Christian, that I would follow God wherever He would take me. And I decided in 2001 that I would follow Aaron Ivey in our marriage as well.

Following Aaron isn't always easy. (Wait, did I just say that?) It's actually less about Aaron and more about me. I'm human and stubborn. Sometimes I want to plant my feet and not move. But following Aaron is also easy because he loves me more than he loves the title "leader." I think I'd like to say that again: my husband loves *me* more than he loves *the title "leader."* Only when a leader loves you more than their position of leadership can you totally trust them. Aaron adores me; he cares for me; he wants the best for me; he sees me as a beautiful woman made by God for big purposes. I trust Aaron and his leadership because his track record proves him to be faithful to God and faithful to me.

But among the reasons why I can follow Aaron well is because many times in our marriage, he has followed *my* lead. (I told you specifically about the one on adoption). The beautiful thing about marriage is that God has unified us as one, and therefore God can and does speak to both of us about decisions and ideas in our marriage. We are both tethered to the Holy Spirit and therefore neither one of us is worried about the other "running the show" or taking advantage of us because we trust God is working in them.

Because of that trust, there have been times in our marriage when we have both said to each other, "I'm not 100 percent on board with what you're saying, but I trust you with this decision." It's not a blind trust; it's not a misinformed trust; it's a trust that knows the other person has our best interest at heart when making these decisions. It's a trust that says "I will *follow* you on this" because I believe your intentions are pure and good and you are listening to God as your ultimate guide.

So let's go back into God's Word, back into Ephesians 5, which lays the groundwork for what marriage should look like as couples following the Lord. You'll recall we've looked at this verse already:

> Wives, submit to your own husbands, as
> to the Lord. For the husband is the head
> of the wife even as Christ is the head of
> the church, his body, and is himself its
> Savior. (Eph. 5:22–23)

This is the verse that can make some women feel unseen, unloved, and less-than. What is clear here is that God is calling on women to follow their own husband just as just as the church follows Christ, its sacrificial and loving Husband. Christ is head over the church (that's us—His people, not the building), and He is also our Savior. But then remember what comes next: "Husbands, love your wives, as Christ loved the church and gave himself up for her" (Eph. 5:25).

There's a calling on our husbands here that would have been odd to the original audience of the Scriptures. The "head" imagery, from back in verse 22, serves as a symbolic picture of what is controlling the body. In the time when this was written, they would see the head (the husband) as being the one in charge, and the body (the wife) laying down her life for the head (the husband). And yet Paul flips this around. He says the husbands (the head) should love their wives (the body) so much that they would give up their life for *HER*. It's a one-eighty from wimpy, weak-willed wife being controlled by my-way-or-the-highway husband.

As Rebecca McLaughlin puts it:

> Complementarian marriage is often summarized as "Wives submit, husbands lead." But this summary doesn't reflect the biblical commands. Wives

are indeed called to submit. But the primary call for husbands is love, and the
additional commands call for empathy
and honor. The command to wives in
Ephesians certainly implies that husbands should lead with the sacrificial
love of Christ. But if we must boil the
Scriptures down, 'Wives submit, husbands love' is a more accurate reflection
of their weight.[9]

Okay then. Submission by the wife should look different to us than what the world (and sometimes, unfor-
tunately, the church) has painted for us. The definition
for submission in the dictionary is this: an act of submitting to the authority or control of another. We have
already talked about a unique calling on a husband's
life from God to lead his family and sacrificially love
his wife. It is here that we as women get to submit to
the authority that God has placed on our husbands.

---

[9] Rebecca McLaughlin, "Confessions of a Reluctant
Complementarian" The Gospel Coalition (September 13,
2018), https://www.thegospelcoalition.org/article/confessions
-reluctant-complementarian/.

To trust his guidance and leadership on our family because God uniquely called him to this.

But a Christian understanding of submission should nuance that dictionary definition up there. We're not submitting to the *control* of our husbands, but to the *love* of our husbands. It's not an authoritarian leader barking orders at us, but a husband who would sacrifice his own life for his bride. The version of leadership where someone looks out for his own good, fights his way to the top, demands respect, and could care less about the people under him is not the type of leader I would ever sign up to follow. And, thank God, it's not the type of headship that God intends for any husband to be.

Instead, we see a gentle leader. A Jesus-like leader. One who would sacrifice his own self so that his wife could flourish. One who would give himself away so that others can succeed. One who washes the feet of those around him.

Now maybe you don't have a husband who is that kind of leader. Few of them are, and none of them is perfect. But as always in life, you and I are ultimately responsible only for ourselves. You can't *make* your husband a gentle, self-sacrificial leader, any more than he can *make* you a respectful, trusting follower. But you can pray for him. You can want what's best for him. You can do everything possible to call him up into that position of love and integrity, "so that even if some do not obey the word, they may be won without a word by the conduct of their wives, when they see your respectful and pure conduct" (1 Pet. 3:1–2). You really can follow him, even when it's hard. You know how I know? Because there are plenty of times Aaron has loved me even when it was hard. He doesn't get to disobey the command to love me just because I happen to be in a bad mood one day. The same goes for me. I don't get to disobey the command to submit to him just because I happen to find him in a moment he's not being husband of the year. We obey these things because *God* calls us to them, not because our spouse demands it.

Jesus is our ultimate example of how a leader leads the people around them well. And as I think about being a leader, and following Aaron as a leader, I want to view everything through the lens of the gospel. I want to both lead *and* follow in a way that looks like Jesus, our ultimate sacrificial, servant leader.

CHAPTER 6

Fight

I hate fighting and conflict. I would rather run from conflict, put my head in the sand with my fingers in my ears, and make myself believe that the conflict is fake. Fighting is perhaps literally my least favorite thing to do. And yet within every relationship you'll ever have on this earth, fighting will be a part of it. There's no way around it. If you tell me you don't have moments of disagreement and arguing and conflict, I might not tell you that you were *lying,* but I would tell you that you aren't *living.* Conflict and fighting are a part of every relationship, including your marriage.

Aaron and I have never been big fighters. Our marriage is fairly easygoing, and neither of us are usually fighting to get our way. But like I said, every relationship has conflict, and so does ours. I don't remember the first time we fought as newlyweds. I would like to say we worked hard to solve it together, whatever it was, and not fight against each other, but I would guess there were hard feelings and hurt feelings surrounding that first fight. I don't remember.

But because of my desire to avoid conflict at all costs, fighting has been a journey for me in marriage. For years I equated fighting with "We're about to get a divorce!" and "This whole thing is over!" Again, very dramatic of me, but also truthful of me. I didn't know how to fight well. I wasn't sure how to enter into conflict knowing we'd be better on the other side of it. I didn't know how to fight *for* Aaron or how to fight *with* Aaron about anything.

> Conflict and fighting are a part of every relationship, including your marriage.

Now I'm not making a judgment about you in what I'm about to say, but it's possible you may be one of those people who actually *enjoys* a little conflict. I had a friend once who admitted she *loved* conflict. After I'd wiped the "what the heck is wrong with you" look off my face and asked her why she would say such a thing, she told me what she really meant was that she liked the *outcome* of conflict. She knew that healthy conflict could and would lead to deeper relationships and a better understanding of the other person.

Okay, I'm still not one to sign up for conflict, but I'll admit that when Aaron and I have entered into a disagreement, argument, conflict, fight—whatever you want to call it—from a healthy perspective, I have seen some of the positive results that my friend was so eagerly anticipating with her love of conflict.

When I think about fighting in marriage, I immediately think of three different ways to fight:

- I see couples fighting against each other.
- I see couples fighting with each other.
- I see couples fighting for each other.

Fighting *against* Your Husband

I like to win. I have never let a small child beat me in Uno just because they're a child. If there's a winner to be crowned, I want that winner to be me. Winning an argument and not having to say "I'm sorry" are sometimes my main priorities whenever I'm going at it with Aaron.

It's gross to think about, but it's been true so many times in our marriage.

I'm not alone in this desire. Francis Chan writes in his book *You and Me Forever,* which he cowrote with his wife, Lisa:

> One verse that keeps us more grounded in this area [fighting] than any other is James 4:6: "God opposes the proud, but gives grace to the humble." For those of us who nurture a win-at-any-cost mentality, this verse should shake us to the core. Only a fool would sacrifice this much for any victory. Let this sink into your brain: God actively fights against the proud person. The pride required to win your argument and defeat your "enemy" provides you with a new opponent: God.[10]

Surprisingly enough then, when you fight against your husband in marriage—and you will!—you have the

---

[10] Francis Chan and Lisa Chan, *You and Me Forever* (San Francisco: Claire Love Publishing, 2014), 69.

opportunity to imitate Christ in your fighting. You have an opportunity to love your husband well, not by laying aside your voice, but by laying aside your pride, becoming humble in your pursuit of reconciliation, knowing that the battle you're fighting against your husband is not the ultimate battle. A real force is at work trying to insert a wedge between you two, and many times it succeeds when it lands in a pride-filled home.

When Aaron and I are fighting *well*—when we're walking through conflict in a healthy manner—we legitimately care about the other person more than we care about being right. For me, it means listening well and not defending my actions. It means hearing what Aaron is feeling and not making it about me. It means trusting his heart even when things feel difficult.

Paul, as usual, said it best, in a verse I've been harping on throughout this book as essential for marriage: "Do nothing from selfish ambition or conceit, but in humility [especially during a fight[11]] count others more significant than yourselves" (Phil. 2:3). When I tell you this is the hardest part of marriage for me, you must remember that I hate conflict, but my sinful heart does love to be

---

[11] I added this part.

right. My flesh loves pointing out someone else's wrongdoings. Every single time I want to fight *against* Aaron,
my flesh wants to become the captain of that ship, and it's
a battle of my soul to throw that captain overboard and
let the Holy Spirit lead me in that conflict.

And yet I have to tell you: some of our most precious
moments in marriage have come after an argument,
when we've both shown up full of humility, when both
of us have laid down our weapons of destruction, and
desired to find a way to become unified on something,
even if it means dying to our own selfish desires.

Dying to ourselves—being "crucified with Christ"
(Gal. 2:20)—is not the easiest thing in the world, and yet
it's exactly what God tells us to do. Many times in marriage we don't feel like staying committed to the truths of
God's Word that tell us when we die to ourselves, Christ
lives in us. But it's true. When we put aside our selfish
desires of the flesh, that's when Christ shines the bright-
est in our lives.

Lisa Whittle says:

> Commitment over mood isn't a slo-
> gan or a trite cliché. It's a hard-fought
> death to self. It's seeing our feelings for

the idols that they are in our lives, rec-
ognizing the times we've put them over
the call of the gospel, and then making the decision to choose Jesus over
everything.[12]

Laying down our idols of victory at whatever cost
takes courage, but your marriage will be better for it.

Fighting *with* Your Husband

When we first moved to Austin in 2008, we were
full of dreams about all the ways God was going to use
our family in this new place. We drove into town in a
big U-Haul with all of our possessions from our nine-
hundred square-foot home in Murfreesboro, Tennessee,
to the three-thousand square-foot home we were renting
in Austin. It was a lot bigger space than we'd been accus-
tomed to living in, and the adjustment to parenting in a
house this size was a little scary. We were parents to four
kids, although only two of them were home with us, as

---

[12] Lisa Whittle, *Jesus Over Everything* (Nashville, TN: W
Publishing Group, 2020), 178.

we were knee-deep in the adoption process of our kids from Haiti.

We had only been in our home a few months when our oldest son, who was four at the time, started having night terrors. If you've never experienced a night terror, it's no biggie because night terrors are not like nightmares, which you remember when you wake up and can recall to anyone who'll listen. You wake up with *no* memory of a night terror; it's the people who watch you having them that call them horrific.

Our son would cry out in the night, and his face would have an abject look of terror like I had never seen before. He seemed so scared. Of *something*. He would scream, "Mommy, Mommy, help me!" even though I was right there holding him as he looked into my face. It was as if he was looking through me while I reassured him I was indeed *right there*! Still, he would continue calling for me with the most frightened look on his face. They were awful.

We researched night terrors and found that many believe they're harmless and may be brought on by extreme exhaustion and fever, among other things. We began to monitor his bedtimes and see if he needed more naps, or anything else we could think of.

One night, my son's night terrors became over-whelming, and I brought him into our bed so he could be next to me if another one came upon him. I was still awake reading in bed, and Aaron was in the backyard with some friends, when my son shot up in bed with the scariest look on his face I had yet to see. He was pointing to a corner of our room and screaming.

To say that I was freaked out would be an understate-ment. I reached out to hold him and try comforting him. But then I did something else: I stared into the corner of the room where he'd been pointing, and I yelled out, "In the name of Jesus, you are *NOT WELCOME* in this house and you must *LEAVE!*" Aaron, hearing the commotion, came sprinting into the house, into our room, and we comforted our son together, looking at each other, won-dering what the world had just happened.

We mentioned the scenario to a few friends, and the consensus was that we were not fighting against flesh and blood here. We were fighting a spiritual force. We were facing the darkness. And it was there, with that insight, that we began a different type of fighting. We began fighting together for our kids and their souls. Friends came over and prayed over every single nook and cranny of our home; they anointed the doorposts with oil; and

Aaron and I prayed bolder prayers than ever before, praying over our kids with new, focused fervor every night before they went to sleep.

I was fighting *with* Aaron against a common enemy. We were fighting this war together.

What is it for you? What are you linking arms for? What kind of need in your home or injustice in our world are you fighting for together, *with* your husband? I remember feeling so close and intimate with Aaron during that time, when we were fighting this spiritual battle for our son while simultaneously fighting to bring our newest kids home from Haiti. We were in it together. My husband was *with* me. And I knew I could fight any battle that came our way, as long as we were fighting it together.

Fighting *for* Your Husband

When I step back and think that God chose me, out of all of the women in the world, to spend my life with Aaron Ivey, my mind is blown away. Do I believe in soul mates? Hmm, I want to, but I'm not so sure. Do I believe there's one person out there for you? Sounds drastic, but I do believe God in His great wonder, infinite knowledge, and complete sovereignty knew that Aaron and I would choose each other and do life together. He wasn't surprised by our union. Even greater than that, He believed that good would come out of us being together.

Therefore, what an honor for me to fight *for* my husband—to be someone in his corner who will be there fighting for him, no matter what life throws at us, no matter what roads we journey down, no matter what sins he gets entangled in. My desire as his wife is not only to love him well, have fun with him, and have an enjoyable companion to do life with, but my desire (and really my honor) as his wife is to be one of the main people in his life who will fight for him.

A few years ago, Aaron entered an extremely difficult season emotionally. He spent hours with our counselor, walking through some deep wounds that he wasn't even aware were there. As his wife, I had a front-row seat to the man he'd become before seeking some counseling support for these issues, and I was there to see the transformation happen within his soul and heart as he worked

> For Aaron to know I'm fighting for him is one of the greatest gifts I could give him.

through these difficult things that had recently surfaced in his life.

But he wasn't alone in our home as he was journeying through all that. I was honored to pray for him, encourage him, and help him remember the ways God had been faithful to him and to us over the years.

As Aaron's wife, not only do I want to be his biggest cheerleader, not only do I want to love him better and be a more constant source of encouragement to him than anyone else on the planet, I want to be the person who cares the most about his soul and his sanctification. For Aaron to know I'm fighting for him is one of the greatest gifts I could give him.

How are you fighting for your husband? Are you praying for him to love God more every day? Are you reminding him of the goodness of God in his life? Are you more concerned that your husband makes it to the end of his life faithfully following Jesus than what your next house is going to look like?

Fighting, conflict, and disagreements are inevitable in the human life. We will all have moments when we're not getting along. We're all alike in that way. But here's where we can separate from the pack. Being someone, or fighting against someone, who is full of pride is a full-blown guarantee for a relationship to crumble, but humility and imitating Jesus are how we learn to fight well within our marriages. They're how we leverage the inevitability of conflict into a net gain, refusing to let our enemy steal from us and opening the door for God to change us, to bless us. Fighting *with* and *for* Aaron are two of my greatest honors in this life. I'd go to battle with that man, and for that man, any day.

CHAPTER 7

Forgive

I finally made my way to one of East Africa's most beautiful countries, Rwanda, in January 2020. I've been intrigued and curious about visiting this country ever since I read the book *Left to Tell* by Immaculée Ilibagiza. In her book, she shares about her life during the genocide where for ninety-one days in 1994, she and seven other Tutsi women hid in the bathroom of a Hutu pastor's house. A million people were slaughtered, strictly because they came from a certain tribe. Families were ripped apart. Neighbors warred against each other. Mothers were murdered in front of their children. The entire country was ravaged, but Immaculée miraculously survived. Her book is one of my all-time favorites, so when I got the opportunity to go to Rwanda, my heart was overjoyed.

But I wasn't quite sure what to expect. Would it feel scary? Desolate? Uncertain? Was it still like the country it had been in the twentieth century? All I know is this: I left there believing in the power of forgiveness, more than from any other example of it I'd ever seen in my life. Obviously I've forgiven people for hurting me. Obviously I've witnessed others' great forgiveness of my own failings. But I have never seen or heard the kind of forgiveness I witnessed while visiting this beautiful country.

In twenty-five years, people of this country have not only rebounded from one of the great injustices of our world, but they are thriving. They're an example of what the power of forgiveness can do in a person, a community, a family, and even a nation. From my short week there, I heard again and again about how they'd been put in positions where they had to make a choice to forgive. Pastor Charles Mugisha[13] spoke with us about the history of Rwanda over dinner one night, and as we asked him how his country has recovered so well, he made a statement that I have yet to forget. He said they had to decide to "quit rehearsing the pain." He explained what the vicious cycle of continuing to live in the pain was

---

[13] https://www.africanewlife.org/about-us/the-founder/

like, and how remaining bitter and unforgiving has a negative effect on people's ability to recover.

I've thought long and hard about that cycle of *rehearsing the pain* he described, and have often wondered how many times it plays out in our marriages— those moments when we choose not only to *remember* the pain (there's nothing wrong with remembering) but to *stay* in the pain. Sit in the pain. Rehearse the pain in our minds. Relive the hell we went through, and ultimately hold that offense—which we said we've already forgiven!—over our husband's head, oftentimes without his even knowing it.

Forgiveness in marriage is difficult but necessary. I've witnessed marriages revived from the dead because of forgiveness. I've witnessed marriages that finally began to thrive because of forgiveness. I've witnessed love come back out of nowhere because of forgiveness. But let's tell the truth now—I've also witnessed marriages crumble because of a lack of forgiveness.

———

A few years ago, Aaron and I were vacationing in St. John's in the Virgin Islands. We love this island and have been there many times. Everything is slower, everything is beautiful, and for a couple in the midst of raising four crazy humans, we thrive when we can get away somewhere where life moves slower.

Most of my memories of being on St. John's involve reading books on the beach, snorkeling with friends, driving around the island in a Jeep with all the windows rolled down, wearing bathing suits I would never wear at home (because it's literally just you and your man on a beach), and spending hours on a boat. But if I was being completely honest, I'd tell you I also have another memory that pops up when I think about our times there.

And it's not a memory that brings me joy.

It actually produces a sick feeling in my stomach, the kind of lump in my throat where I might just start to cry even though I'm trying not to. It doesn't involve swimming, reading, or lying on the beach. It involves Aaron and I sitting on the bed in the house we were renting, looking over our calendars for the next semester, and getting into a fight over our upcoming work trips.

Here, I'll lay it all out for you. (Deep breath.) Aaron said something to me in that moment that hurt me deeply. It isn't worth rehashing exactly what it was, because what he said is not the point of this story. The point is this:

Aaron hurt me with his words. And I can still remember the color of the flowers on the comforter we were sitting on. I remember the exact way we were sitting on the bed. I remember the screened-in porch that was attached to our room. Most of all, I remember the way he made me feel in that moment.

By the time it was all over, we were able to work through our disagreement. Aaron apologized and I forgave him. At least I thought I forgave him. I mean, I *said* I forgave him, and life moved on. We enjoyed the rest of our vacation, spent many more hours at the beach, ate a lot of good food, and then came home to our regular lives again. Except that a few years later, this conversation popped back into my head while we were once again having a similar discussion at home about our work/travel life. All of a sudden, I not only was hurt all over again by something that had happened years ago, but I was also holding that earlier conversation over his head again—the one that Aaron apologized for; the one I supposedly forgave. I was projecting his previous mistake on him now as if he'd said the same words to me again. Which he had not.

I remember feeling insecure and angry all at once, wondering where those feelings were coming from.

Not until later did I realize what I'd done. I had taken something that happened years ago and relived it. I had stepped right back into that bedroom in St John's and acted like Aaron was hurting me with his words all over again. Except that I *wasn't* in that bedroom, Aaron *wasn't* saying it again, and we had supposedly dismissed that disagreement years ago.

There is so much danger in unforgiveness. So much danger and so much devil. And when I stepped back from my own "rehearsing the pain" moment that day, I knew I'd just been given a wakeup call.

Aaron and I both travel in our jobs, and the root of bitterness I was feeling was being fueled by my inability to forgive him for how he'd hurt me when the conflict over our schedules came up on vacation. I knew if I wasn't careful, I would keep holding Aaron accountable for that offense every single time the subject of traveling was brought up, which was unfair to him on so many levels. My inability to truly forgive him would put a wedge of bitterness between the two of us.

> There is so much danger in unforgiveness.

Truth is, it had been a small moment in time. What's more, it wasn't any worse than anything I've ever done to him. He had messed up, he knew it, and he had genuinely apologized. It should be *over* with me by now. But if I left it unattended, that seed of unforgiveness would keep growing in me, deeper and deeper, until one day I'd look up and realize my inability to truly forgive was costing me intimacy with him. Every time we'd talk about our schedules, I would be defensive. Every time we'd talk about work travel, I would be insecure. Every time we'd talk about which one of us needed to make an adjustment, I would be mad at him if it was me—all because of a few words he said years earlier that he has apologized for and I've told him I forgave him.

Apparently, I hadn't. And God began to stir in my heart the fact that I was holding on to this pain and using it against my husband in a way that was detrimental to our intimacy. It was as if I was holding on to a flame that Aaron thought we'd extinguished long ago, and yet I was allowing it to burn us every time we talked about it.

Unforgiveness was hurting my heart and my marriage.

Perhaps the pain and hurt feelings I've just described seems like a walk in the park compared to some of the conflicts you've experienced (or are experiencing) in your marriage. You're thinking of the pain you're dealing with and wishing your biggest hurts were only a few unintended harsh words. Let me tell you, I get that. But I also want to tell you that I have witnessed God work miracles in marriages through forgiveness. Two couples that I love dearly have walked through infidelity in their marriages. They've endured things that no one should need to walk through with a loved one. They should not be married today, and yet their marriages are not only intact, but thriving.

The saving grace in their marriages has been *forgiveness*. As Corrie ten Boom said, "Forgiveness is an act of the will—not an emotion."[14] When we are hurt by someone we love, our emotions are real. They aren't lying to us. They just aren't what we should base our ability to forgive on. Because if our emotions were any indicators of whether or not we should forgive, we never would.

In Corrie ten Boom's book *Tramp for the Lord*, she describes an encounter she had while speaking at a church in Munich, where she came face-to-face with a

---

[14] Eric Metaxas, *7 Women and the Secrets of Their Greatness* (Nashville, TN: Nelson Books, 2015), 136.

former guard from her time at the Ravensbrück concentration camp. The man approached her after her talk, and told her he'd become a Christian since the war. He said he knew that God had forgiven him, and asked if she would forgive him as well. While he waited for her to shake his hand, Corrie said she "wrestled with the most difficult thing I have ever had to do. For I had to do it—I knew that. The message that God forgives has a prior condition: that we forgive those who have injured us."[15] But can you imagine? After everything this man and the regime he represented had done to her? What they'd taken from her? Her sister? Her father? The happy life she'd always known? But she did it. She shook his hand. She did forgive him.

Forgiveness frees us.

This level of forgiveness seems so grand compared to my daily forgiving of my husband when he wrongs me. But the truth is that when we are hurt, we are hurt. Of course there are varying levels for our hurt, but nonetheless forgiveness is needed for healing to occur.

---

[15] Corrie ten Boom, *Tramp for the Lord* (Grand Rapids, MI: Fleming H. Revell Co., 1974), 54.

When I've talked to women who've forgiven their husband for having an affair,[16] I often hear the same sentiment from them: "How could I not?" Seems crazy if you think about it, because our flesh screams, "OF COURSE NOT! HE CHEATED ON YOU!" But then the Spirit reminds us of everything God did to forgive us. The Spirit reminds us of what great lengths the Father went to bring us back to Him.

Our flesh screams, NO!—and the Spirit says, "How can I not?"

I desire so deeply within me for my marriage to model the freedom that God has granted us through His forgiveness. I want to be a wife who forgives her husband of wrongdoings, not just because she thinks she should and doesn't want to rock the boat, but because she wants to be a wife who sacrificially and willingly forgives him when he asks for it. I want to be the kind of wife and woman who always remembers that my grievances toward the Lord are greater than anything Aaron could ever do toward me, and yet in God's great kindness, He still chooses to forgive me.

---

[16] Which if we're honest feels like the greatest pain our husbands could put on us.

As Lysa TerKeurst says, "Feelings are indicators, not dictators. They can indicate where your heart is in the moment, but that doesn't mean they have the right to dictate your behavior and boss you around."[17] As wives, we have God's Word to stand on (and boss us around) when it comes to forgiveness, and not our feelings alone. When we pull back and realize that God has forgiven us of so much, how could we not forgive our husbands?[18] For *anything*?

As I think about the beautiful smiles and faces of the people of Rwanda as they talked about their journey through forgiveness, and I remember Corrie Ten Boom's words as she forgave the man responsible for so many deaths, including her sister Betsie, I can't help but think of the importance of forgiveness within our marriages. Without forgiveness there is no hope, no redemption, and no healing within relationships. Not all of these faults can be forgotten, but not one of these relationships

---

[17] Lysa TerKeurst, *Unglued: Making Wise Choices in the Midst of Raw Emotions* (Grand Rapids, MI: Zondervan, 2012), 98.

[18] Just so we are clear about this—forgiveness does *not* mean allowing yourself to stay in an abusive relationship.

will thrive in this lifetime without the Holy Spirit guiding them toward forgiveness.

Some of the moments in my marriage where I have felt the most cared for, the most loved, and the most cherished have been moments when I have asked Aaron for forgiveness, and he has looked me straight in the eyes and granted it to me. Sure, his emotions were wounded, but by the Spirit of God in him, he was able to grant me forgiveness—not because he's an amazing human being,[19] but because he realizes how much he, too, has been forgiven by his Father.

"Be kind to one another, tenderhearted, forgiving one another, as God in Christ forgave you" (Eph. 4:32). God through Christ has forgiven us completely, and not for one moment does He throw our sins against Him back in our faces. Let us be wives who forgive completely and without holding our husbands' sins against them any longer than God has held ours against us. By the help of the Holy Spirit, we can forgive fully.

And quit rehearsing the pain.

---

[19] Although I do think he's an amazing human being!

CHAPTER 8

Sex

You've probably picked up on the fact that I forget a lot of the details in marital moments with Aaron. With twenty years behind us, the moments can sometimes blur together. But I actually remember the first time Aaron and I had sex. Obviously I'm not going to tell you about it, but I will tell you this: *it was on our wedding night*. Yes, we were sexually pure in our relationship until our wedding night, which was actually a great accomplishment for both of us. This doesn't make us better than anyone else, but it's something we're proud of, because we worked hard to stay true to what God's Word says is best for His people and their sexuality.

When Aaron and I started dating, I was fresh off an eleven-month new relationship with Jesus. Although I grew up in a Christian home, walked down the aisle in third grade, and was baptized, my relationship and love for God didn't develop until I was twenty-one years old and on the other side of some hard trials in life. My new dating relationship with Aaron was sent straight from God to me, and our relationship was like none I'd ever experienced.

Up until I started dating Aaron, I had never been pure in a dating relationship before. I had never held purity in high regard, the purity that God (by His mercy, and for our good) asks of His people. The fact that I had messed up so many other times in my life kept me from seeing the good in ever trying to stay pure. It felt impossible. In fact, it felt of no use to me until Aaron and I began dating.

> I brought tons of baggage into our marriage, and most of it centered on my past sexual sin prior to dating Aaron.

I remember wondering many times in our dating relationship if Aaron truly loved me. He *told* me he loved me. He treated me as though he loved me. He talked and acted like he loved me. Yet we weren't having sex, and so I wasn't quite sure . . . because for so many years, sex equaled love to me. And now all of a sudden, there was no sex, and yet a lot of love.

I brought tons of baggage into our marriage, and most of it centered on my past sexual sin prior to dating Aaron. I unpacked that baggage and got rid of most of it, but even today after following Jesus for two decades and being married for almost that whole time, remnants of my baggage can still make their way into my home and into our marriage.

I grew up in what some might call the "purity culture" of the church. Christian author Joe Carter describes it this way:

> "Purity culture" is the term often used for the evangelical movement that attempts to promote a biblical view of purity by discouraging dating and promoting virginity before marriage, often through the use of tools such as purity pledges, symbols such as purity rings, and events such as purity balls.[20]

---

[20] Joe Carter, "The FAQs: What You Should Know about Purity Culture," The Gospel Coalition (July 24, 2019),

Side note here: please get a new name for "purity balls." But none of this language is unfamiliar to me, because the church culture I grew up in was all over it. My dad took me out to dinner one night when I was a young adolescent and presented me with a locket to wear around my neck to symbolize the key to my heart and my sexual purity. My parents' hope was that I would stay sexually pure until marriage, and this necklace was that symbol. The problem with purity for me, and for so many others, is that we weren't sure why we were staying pure or who we were staying pure for.

For me as a high schooler, I was convinced I would marry every guy I ever dated. (Seems so dumb to me now as a forty-year-old but, gosh, it felt real at the moment.) And since I was sure we'd eventually marry, it wasn't a top priority for me to save myself for them. Sex didn't seem sacred to me as a teenager. It seemed normal for two people to have sex who loved each other the way I thought I loved my boyfriends.

So about the only thing the purity culture did for many of us was leave us in a dreaded sense of guilt and

---

https://www.thegospelcoalition.org/article/faqs-know-purity-culture/.

confusion over sex. There was such a huge emphasis on staying pure and not having sex until you're married (which is good and right, of course), but there was a lack of why this all matters and how the virtue of purity transfers into your marriage. I've met so many women my age who saved themselves sexually for marriage, married their dream guy, but found sex such a disappointment to them for different reasons. I've also met more women than I can count who enjoyed sex as a single girl, and yet sex within a covenant marriage with their husband became dreadful, and they wished they could experience the excitement of single sex again. The problem with purity culture wasn't that it promoted virginity, per se, but that it created a massive expectation that sex within marriage would be perfect, care-free, and full of fireworks. Good sex was painted as the reward for staying pure—and that's not the way the Bible presents sex.

As a follower of Jesus, we know the Bible is quite clear about our sexual purity. We are to "abstain from sexual immorality; that each one of you know how to control his own body in holiness and honor" (1 Thess. 4:3–4). But what does that mean for us in marriage?

———

Aaron and I had only been married for a few years when an older woman, sharing with a small group of us, was recalling the night when she found out her father had passed away. She talked about the pain she felt, being told over the phone that her dad was gone. Many tears were shed that night in the retelling of her story. I was so sad for her. But as she continued, I became really intrigued by what she said next. She disclosed to us that she and her husband, after hearing about losing her father, had made love that night, and how healing it had been to her broken heart. The intimacy they shared that night had ministered peace and strength to her in her weakened, hurting, damaged, grief-stricken emotional state.

As a relative newlywed at the time, who enjoyed sex with her husband, and had sex with him often, the fact that this woman made love to her husband the night she was so saddened by the death of her dad was a mystery to me. It didn't make sense to me. It honestly felt a little weird to me.

Over time, as life would have it, Aaron and I ventured out of that newlyweds-have-awesome-sex-whenever-and-wherever-we-want-it lifestyle. And the older I got, and the more life I lived, I began to see more clearly what this woman had meant when she spoke those words to us years before. She was explaining that the intimacy between a husband and wife is a bonding of their hearts, souls, and bodies. What I didn't know then, that I do know now, is that life is hard. Marriage is hard. Parenting is hard. Middle age is hard. And yet God in His graciousness toward us has offered men and women a way to experience intimacy inside their marriage that is unique only to them.

I can get many things from people who aren't my partner in life. I can get emotional support somewhere else—from my counselor or friends. I can get physical support somewhere else—at the gym or the doctor's office. I can get help with parenting and paying my mortgage. I can even travel with others, with various groups of people. But no one else can fulfill my sexual desires other than Aaron within our marriage. *No one.* He's the only person in the world who gets to be a part of that in my life.

When we think about sex as this beautiful gift that God has granted husbands and wives, it helps us evaluate the gravity of it in our own marriages. Perhaps this chapter scares you because you don't enjoy sex. You're tired. You aren't fulfilled. Sex is boring. You feel uncomfortable with your body. Or perhaps you desire sex more than your husband does, and it makes you feel like a freak (which you aren't, by the way). Or perhaps the demands of life have taken control of your marriage, and sex seems like a thing of the past.

But what if we reevaluated what sex looks likes in our marriages? How would it change the intimacy that you do or don't feel with your husband? For me personally, I still enjoy sex and have not become the stereotypical wife who claims to have a headache in order to fall asleep without having sex first. But I'd be lying if I said I don't still have some old thought patterns associated with sex. Sometimes instead of viewing sex as a gift from God, I can't seem to keep from viewing it as an indicator of how much Aaron loves me. I hate when I feel that.

What I mean is, if I want to have sex, but for whatever reason Aaron doesn't, I don't need to receive it as a rejection. I just need to show him grace and not overthink whatever emotion he might be feeling, knowing the many times I've felt the same way. It doesn't mean he's falling out of love with me. Yet somehow, this is a battle I keep having to fight. We could have had sex two days earlier, but in that moment, I allow old ideas of sex to enter into my brain and convince me that Aaron no longer loves me and has another family in another state that he's also caring for.[21]

Oh, to be free of what my enemy knows can still torment me.

———

There have been seasons in our marriage when sex was plentiful—the few years before kids, and even the years when our kids were younger. Although those were tiring days of parenting four kids all under ten, Aaron and I could still find alone time at night by 7:30 after we put the kids down.[22] Today, of course, as parents to four teenagers, alone time is much harder to come by. The kids are sometimes up later than *we* are, and there are few nights of the week when we aren't running around from activity to activity with one or all of them.

There have also been seasons when sex was more enjoyable than others. Bodies change, hormones change, our health changes. There have been seasons when one of us wanted to have sex more than the other, seasons

---

[21] I tend to be dramatic.

[22] I'm a big fan of early bedtime for kids!

when mental health struggles made it difficult to desire sex, seasons when sex has felt sexy and fun, and seasons when sex has felt boring and mundane.

But in any of these seasons, in *all* of these seasons, we need to remind ourselves what sex really is. Otherwise, I'll make it all about *me*. He'll make it all about *him*. It won't serve its complementary role in our marriage.

So what is it? It's fundamentally a gift from God. Something He cares about. Something He wants us to enjoy, and something He gives us to point to an even greater, more fulfilling enjoyment—intimacy with Him.

The good news is that God is not missing from our sexuality and our sex lives. He cares so much about our sexuality because He cares so much about us. He created us as sexual beings, and He instilled pleasure into the act of lovemaking because He cares about the entirety of our physical and emotional makeup—mind, soul, and body. What this knowledge should do for us is to make this aspect of our marriage feel like a safe place, realizing the

> God is not missing from our sexuality and our sex lives. He cares so much about our sexuality because He cares so much about us.

God of the universe who created the marriage bond also created our bodies in a such a way that they fit together when we have sex. He's thought of everything. Nothing has been neglected. He cares about this part of your life, just like He cares about every other part of your life.

That's why He created sex and sexual desire to be expressed exclusively in the lifelong covenant of marriage between a man and a woman. *Because that's what's best for us.* That's where we can share it and experience it with total purity and freedom. That's where sex becomes a gift, not a god. And make no mistake, sex makes a terrible god.

As I've said before, oftentimes people go into marriage hoping it will fix them or complete them. Maybe you're one who waited to have sex, expecting sex and marriage to make you ultimately happy. Or maybe your romantic life has been complicated with terrible relationships, and you're longing to place all your hope in this man and this relationship for every bit of your emotional satisfaction and fulfillment. The truth is that only God can do that for you and me. We ultimately were not made for sex or marriage. We were made for God. He is the only one who can complete us and satisfy us fully, who can fulfill those deep holes within our hearts for the intimacy and acceptance we crave. That's too much pressure to expect our husbands to be able to bear for us. It's putting a burden on them that they can't carry and were never meant to carry. And the same could be said in reverse—this is too much pressure for them to put on us, too. We can't be our husbands' god any more than they can be ours.

> God in His grace and kindness has created a unique connection of intimacy between husband and wife that cannot be replicated in any other human relationship.

And yet when placed in God's hands—with gratitude, with understanding, with appreciation for His allowing us to share this kind of intimacy with one person, with our husband—sex becomes an aspect of marriage that is not only ours to share, but is ours to weather together as well.[23]

It's part of figuring each other out.

---

[23] While sex is a journey that you and your husband will journey together, there's nothing wrong with seeing a counselor or medical doctor about any emotional or physical struggles within your marriage and your sex life.

Learning each other is a lifelong journey that you and your husband get to embark on. After having sex with the same man for almost two decades, I can attest that even with the many changes we've experienced through all these seasons of marriage, it just keeps getting better and better with every year we spend together. We have a lifetime to discover each other's bodies, each other's likes and dislikes, each other's comforts and pleasures. Lore Ferguson Wilbert says, "The first time you have sex with your spouse is never as fully satisfying as the one-hundredth or the thousandth. We remember the curves, the spaces, the familiar aches, the pleasures, the small signs of build-up, and the crashing release."[24] Your sexual journey with your husband is unique. Fascinating. It's a most personal exercise in complementing each other.

I'm not naïve about the struggles that can become wrapped up in your sex life. If it makes you feel better, we've struggled too in certain seasons. Struggling with your sex life doesn't mean you aren't meant to be together anymore. It also doesn't mean your relationship

---

[24] Lore Ferguson Wilbert, *Handle with Care: How Jesus Redeems the Power of Touch in Life and Ministry* (Nashville, TN: B&H Publishing, 2020), 115.

is doomed. No matter if you enjoy sex with your husband, or you dread the night on the calendar when you know it's going to happen,[25] none of it negates the truth that God in His grace and kindness has created a unique connection of intimacy between husband and wife that cannot be replicated in any other human relationship. There's a fight to be had for this part of your marriage. Sex is not the ultimate goal in marriages, but it is one of God's gifts to us to bind us together. It tells a beautiful story—one we need to remember often.

---

[25] Yes, if you are a newlywed or not yet married, there will be a day when you look at your husband and say, "Thursday, yes, that night works for me," while planning your meals for the week and who will pick up the kids from soccer and get them to dance class. It's not ideal, I know. But it does happen in a lot of marriages to prioritize sexual health through those wildly busy patches of life!

CHAPTER 9

Parent

I never imagined my life not having kids in it. It's always been a dream of mine to be a mama. And although I wouldn't call myself the most hands-on mom there's ever been, I'm honored that God chose me to do life with my four kids.

Parenting will go down in history as probably the most difficult job I've ever done. I never expected myself to say that, because I always assumed mothering would be a walk in the park. But now here I am, seventeen years into this parenting gig, and I realize more every day that I am completely incapable of doing this job well, apart from the help of God.

I want to say something really quick before we move forward in this idea of complementing each other through parenting. I realize you may be one of those women who is doing this job alone. You're a single parent, for whatever reason—doesn't really matter how it happened. All that matters is that you're the only one doing the disciplining now, the only one making meals, the only one coordinating schedules, the only one doing it all. Let me just acknowledge you before we move on, so that you don't think I don't see you in this world, since this chapter will talk about how a husband and wife can complement each other in the area of parenting. I *do* see you, and I hope something I say will be used by the Spirit of God to speak strength and comfort to you in the enormous, heroic task you wake up to undertake each morning.

I would not be the parent I am today without Aaron walking this road with me. Since we're different in other areas of our lives, we are also different in our parenting skills and perspectives. One of the beautiful things that God does when He places a man and a woman in a marriage is that He creates their family right then and there, differences and all. Aaron and I began our family unit the day we said, "I do," not knowing what the rest of our years would look like, whether we would have kids or not to add to this family.

In God's perfect plan we are now the proud parents to four beautiful children who all joined our family differently. Three of them joined us through various means of adoption, as I've said, and one through the old-school biological route. As we have been parenting over the years, I've seen firsthand the way God brings out the best in each parent and how we must truly work together or else we'll fail miserably. I've also seen my worst sins and coping mechanisms come to the surface through parenting. The same could be said for Aaron. Thankfully, parenting provides us a unique way of helping each other fight those specific sin struggles together.

It also keeps us humble.

As we all remember, 2020 went down as the year of mayhem. COVID-19 stormed into our world and quickly took over the entire globe. It had all of us locked in our homes for weeks upon weeks. Even just reading about it again here possibly makes you recall the hardness of those months and wonder how we all made it through. Millions of jobs were lost, hundreds of thousands of *lives* were lost, and everyday normal things were halted around the world.

As we ventured through those first weeks of trying to figure out life as two working parents, plus four kids who were now essentially homeschooled, it looked messy at times. Aaron and I were still in the process of trying to figure out if we were supposed to really be teaching them or if they could manage on their own, when I went into full-on "Mom-will-get-us-all-on-track" mode and created a schedule for us all. I spent hours figuring out how to make sure all the kids had an equal amount of time in the day for the computers they were all sharing. I made sure each kid had a device to use for the 8,490 Zoom calls they had with their teachers and classmates every day. I included time for reading,[26] chores, workouts, and even time to sit on their behinds and watch TV each day. I felt on top of the world when I finally finished that schedule, and I could not wait to present it to my family. I was expecting to hear praises from my people when they saw how much I cared about them in this unsteady time of homeschooling life that we never signed up for.

You probably know where this is going, don't you? I walked into the kitchen with a spreadsheet in hand, got some tape to put it on the fridge, and asked everyone

---

[26] Yes, I still ask my kids to read each day, though I would bet my whole life they only read when I remind them. But I feel really good about myself for putting it on the schedule!

to gather around. I then began to remind them that we were now a homeschool family that included two work-from-home parents as well, and so Mom had saved the day with a schedule that would keep us all on track. I could imagine the cheers building up in them as they reviewed my handiwork.

Except that no one cheered. No one high-fived me. No one even thanked me. Everyone stared at me for about 4.7 seconds, and then the complaining began. Not one child wanted a schedule to keep them on track. No one wanted to be told when they could watch television each day, and the computer schedule nearly put one of my kids completely over the edge. I felt defeated, as if my hours of work were very much underappreciated and undervalued.

I immediately began to believe the lie that Aaron really *was* the better parent. Because he is way more fun than me. He is way more likely to say yes to making cookies at night. He would drop everything and take all of them to Sonic for ice cream any time of day. I, on the other hand, am way more likely to monitor bedtimes. I'm concerned about their sugar intake. I like for things to be done in an orderly fashion. I make sure everyone is playing outside each day during the summer months. I'm the one getting the emails from their teachers, and I'm the one telling them that "readers are leaders," so *get to reading*! Not one time has Aaron ever developed a schedule for the kids.

But I stuck to that schedule. And we began our new quarantine routines, even if some of them hated it, even if they despised the idea of only having one hour a day for TV time, even if they wished they were in a different family where there were no guidelines or schedules taped to the fridge.

And you know what? After a few weeks had gone by, I began to notice something about our family. We were in a groove. Things were working more smoothly now than during the first week of homeschool. Computers were being easily shared, and kids were getting their work done efficiently and on time.

How do you like *that*? Maybe the un-fun parent had a place around here after all.

On a family walk one night, my oldest son and I were bringing up the rear, and I asked him the question that probably was just my way of fishing for a few words of encouragement from him. I said, "Do you think I'm a good mom?" He stopped in his tracks, appalled at my question, and proclaimed, "Yes, you're a *great* mom." I asked him why he thought so. I might have even confessed to him that I sometimes wish I was more fun, like Dad.

That's when he said something I'll never forget: "Mom," he said, "if it weren't for you, this house wouldn't function very well." And, you know, without sounding too braggy, I think that's true. I do help this house function well, even in the way I parent the kids, even where I'm more of a complement to Aaron's way of parenting them.

Especially in my spreadsheet making.

———

There's a tendency in parenting to forget that you're indeed teammates working toward the same goal. We often refer to our family of six as Team Ivey, which I like because this metaphor makes Aaron and I sound like sort of the *coaches* of this team. And if we keep going with this metaphor, what we see here is that the coaches of the best performing teams in whatever sport you may be watching bring different gifts and skill sets to the team they're leading.

When I start to forget that Aaron and I are on the same team, that's when I start to think his gifts and skills are the better ones and that I'm not needed, that he's the fun parent and I'm the strict parent. Which, let me just add, could not be further from the truth. I am fun as well. Ask anybody. And though Aaron is not what you'd call a tough disciplinarian, none of his kids would want to disobey their dad.

Complementing each other in parenting is where the beauty happens in a home. What my children are getting from us are two unique parents utilizing our giftings in the unique ways that God has created us. Without running the risk of taking God's Word out of context, I can't help but think of it as being similar to the encouragement Paul gave the church in Corinth about cherishing all the different ways that God had gifted them.

> If the whole body were an eye, where would be the sense of hearing? If the whole body were an ear, where would be the sense of smell? But as it is, God arranged the members in the body, each one of them, as he chose. If all were a single member, where would the body be? As it is, there are many parts, yet one body. (1 Cor. 12:17–20)

We see here that Paul is talking about the church of God. The people that make up the church are different people who are gifted at different things, but they are all following Jesus. And Paul's point is that we *need them all*. No one is greater or of more use; they all have a purpose within the body.

If this is true for God's big family, the church, then it's certainly true for individual families! I see this so much in parenting. God has put your family together and created something beautiful that only He can. I wonder how much better of a team we would all be if we valued each other's unique giftings instead of wishing to be more like our husband, or despising our husband for not being more like us. When I look at Team Ivey and the dad that Aaron is, I want to love what he brings to the family. The way he can make us all laugh is a gift he brings to us, in his own unique and beautiful style. The way he speaks to our sons and instills worth in them is something I can't do with the same exact brand of effectiveness. The way he couldn't care less, when our daughter was younger, whether her clothes matched when she went out, was a gift to her and to our family.

We have a unique opportunity together with our kids. There are no other people who get to pour into them and their lives the way that we do, and I'm thankful our parenting styles can be different and still be good and unified.

Parenting is *truly* a complementary exercise.

But let me close by talking about another kind of uniqueness that comes into play in parenting which, for good or for ill, teaches them lessons they'll need throughout their lives. As Aaron and I journey through parenting together, we give our kids a front-row seat to see two broken, sinful people, both of whom are trying to follow Jesus with all that we have. They're watching us in everything that we do. They see the Aaron and Jamie that no one else sees. They see the people who don't stand on stages. They see the people who aren't on the podcast. They see the things that don't make the insides of a book. They see the people who screw up when disciplining their children. They see the people who argue and fight when things don't go their way. They see the parents who mess up in parenting, and they also see the people who ask for forgiveness, from each other and from their kids. They see the parents who fight and then apologize and reconcile. They see the people who kiss and are affectionate in the kitchen at the end of the day. They see the people who cry when they worship Jesus. They see the people who spend time in God's Word because it is bread to their souls.

Our kids see all of us. The good, the bad, and the ugly. They also see two people chasing Jesus on the good days and the bad days. Our kids see the ministry of God in our lives. What a gift to give them. As we parent them.

> Our kids see all of us. The good, the bad, and the ugly.

Invest in your own home team. And cheer each other on as each of you parents your children in your own unique way.

CHAPTER 10

Mission

I get all mushy when I think about the kindness of God in letting me do life with Aaron. I mean, let's be honest. In the entire world there are roughly 7.8 billion people,[27] with scientists estimating that a little over half of them are men. If my math is right (and there's a good chance it's not), this means there are roughly 3.9 billion men in the world, and God in His wisdom thought it best for Aaron Ivey to marry Jamie Beakley.

This still blows my mind.

As I've thought about and written each chapter of this book, I've caught myself thinking whichever chapter I was writing at the time was the most important in our marriage. I might have even thought it more than a

---

[27] https://www.worldometers.info/world-population/

few times. But for the sake of ending this book on a high note, I'd like to make my third and final answer that I really do believe *this* chapter—about being on mission with your spouse—is perhaps the most important aspect of a healthy, thriving, loving, Christ-honoring marriage.

The truth of the whole "mission" thing is that Jesus left the earth and challenged us to be on mission for Him. Before you get confused by that language, let me clear something up. Being on mission does not equal being a *missionary*. Think instead of all the movies you've watched with the word *Mission* in the title. Think of all the movies you've watched where someone embarks on a mission.

> Being on mission with your spouse means you're each running your own race toward the same finish line.

Being on mission with your spouse means you're each running your own race toward the same finish line. Your end game is the same. You desire the same thing. You believe in the same things. And even if you're cringing right now because this doesn't describe you and your spouse at all, it doesn't need to stay like that forever. Let me explain.

Aaron and I are asked quite often, "How do you do it?" We often respond with, "Do *what*?" Then the person usually says something like this: "How do you both do your careers and still support each other. How do you stay on the same page about things?" We know what they're asking. They're saying, "You seem to have different goals in life. Aaron is a pastor and songwriter, and Jamie talks for a living. Those don't seem to be on the same mission page."

But I would like to disagree. Aaron and I have been on the same mission since June 22, 2001, when we said, "I do" and combined our lives together as one. Our mission comes straight from the mouth of Jesus as He left His disciples, where He said to them:

> "Go therefore and make disciples of all nations, baptizing them in the name of the Father and of the Son and of the Holy Spirit, teaching them to observe all that I have commanded you. And behold, I am with you always, to the end of the age." (Matt. 28:19–20)

With everything we have ever done or will ever do, we have one mission: to make great the name of Jesus and teach those around us all the ways God has taught us to follow Him. Everything goes back to that statement right there. When Aaron and I get to the end of our lives and we die in our bed together while holding hands— just let me believe this will be our ending, okay?—I hope we can say to each other that we did just that. That we made disciples. That we lifted high the name of Jesus. That we taught those around us what it looks like to run hard after Him.

Now before you get all upset with me and say things like, "Jamie, you and Aaron both work in ministry; being on mission is your job!" I want you to know this is not our mission in life because Aaron works for a church and I host a Christian podcast. The reason it's our mission in life is because we are followers of Jesus—just like *you* (I hope) are a follower of Jesus.

I will never forget something Aaron said to me when I was throwing around the idea of starting my own podcast. I had been in radio for a hot minute here in Austin[28] and was thinking I'd like to do my own thing with a podcast. I brainstormed a few ideas and finally knew I'd hit

---

[28] I tell this whole story in my book *You Be You*, if you're interested in how I ended up on the radio.

on a great concept for a new show. I marched my proud self into our living room and announced to Aaron that I had the perfect idea for my very first podcast. I was giddy with excitement and couldn't wait to see him giddy with me.

I laid it out to him with all my excitement and eagerly awaited his response. There's no need rehashing the whole podcast idea, except to tell you I'd imagined a podcast where a friend and I would recap a certain reality TV show and put our views and opinions out there for the world to enjoy. I felt the idea was brilliant and could see it taking off instantly.

As soon as I finished with my whole spiel, Aaron looked at me and, without skipping a beat, asked me this one question that I've never forgotten. He said, "Since when do we do things with our lives that don't have kingdom value?"

Mic drop.

I paused and tried to hold back my tears because my most brilliant, perfect idea[29] had just been smashed to pieces on the rug of our living room. I think I said

---

[29] I have friends who do this exact thing in their podcast, and it's awesome.

something like, "Why do you have to be such a pastor right now? Can't you just support me in my ideas?" and stormed off like any super mature adult would do.

After a few tears, and after realizing he wasn't being my pastor but was simply being my partner on this mission we've dedicated ourselves to following, I knew he was right. Everything we've ever done in life has been all for the mission that Jesus left us to live for at the end of the book of Matthew, right before He ascended to the right hand of the Father.

Everything we've ever done. All for the mission.

- Moving to Tennessee with no money and barely a job?

    It was *all for the mission.*

- Aaron getting a job at Starbucks in the middle of traveling full-time?

    All for the mission.

- Me staying home with our babies when they were little?

    All for the mission.

- Aaron taking a job at The Austin Stone Community Church?

    All for the mission.

- Me quitting my job at the radio station?[30]

  All for the mission.

- Me starting the podcast that I produce and host now?

  All for the mission.

- Us having people sit around our table for dinner?

  All for the mission.

- Me traveling around the world telling people about Jesus?

  All for the mission.

- Us opening our home to a medically fragile child from Haiti for nine weeks?

  All for the mission.

You can get caught up in thinking that this "all for the mission" talk is for those who work for the church, in the church, or in church settings, and you couldn't be more wrong. Aaron and I are on the same team—as *believers,* not as people in ministry—and the last I checked, teammates always have the same goal. The prize. We are

---

[30] Again, it's in the other book.

running the race that is set before us, and we are looking to Jesus as our guide (Heb. 12:2) in everything we do. If Aaron were to take a job in a corporate setting tomorrow, and I would become a teacher tomorrow, nothing about our mission would change. Nothing.

Pastor and author Ray Ortlund said it best, I think, how when you get married and become "one flesh," you're now *one* in everything: "one story, one purpose, one reputation, one bed, one suffering, one budget, one family."[31] Aaron and I are indeed one, and that means our mission in life must also be one.

———

I have been beyond blessed to travel to Africa a few times in my life and go on two safaris in two different countries. The first safari I went on was in Kenya; the second was in Rwanda. Both of them were quite different, and if you're ever asked if you want to go on a safari in Africa, the answer should always be yes.

I remember in Kenya, at the Maasai Mara National Reserve, looking out over the land and seeing animals living together, doing the things that animals do. This

[31] Ray Ortland, *Marriage and the Mystery of the Gospel* (Wheaton, IL: Crossway, 2016), 30.

is what feels right for them. I'll never be able to see the elephants in a zoo again and think they are where they're supposed to be, because I've seen an elephant in the wild, and *that's* where they're supposed to be. But this isn't a story about zoos or safari animals; it's about something our guide told us on both of these adventures.

Of all the animal facts our guide threw at us that day in Kenya,[32] there is one fact I wrote down in my phone notes that I continue to think about. He told us tons of stuff about hippos and zebras and giraffes, but his comment about the warthogs is the one that stuck with me. He said warthogs, when they're being chased, forget why they're running, and then they get eaten. Think Pumbaa from *The Lion King* if you need a visual for warthogs! They're just running along, probably away from a predator, and then all of a sudden they forget why they're running. They *stop* running. And then they end up being eaten by whatever was chasing them from the beginning.

I remember in that moment, instantly relating this idea to the Christian life and to a verse you might be familiar with: "Be sober-minded; be watchful. Your adversary the devil prowls around like a roaring lion, seeking someone to devour" (1 Pet. 5:8).

---

[32] Both safari guides told us the same things, so it must be true, right?!

I'd like to make a bold statement here, and since I'm one of the authors of this book, I can do it, so here I go. If you are in a marriage and you forget why you're running, the devil will pounce on your marriage like a lion until he's killed it. When men and women in a covenant marriage—who are meant to *complement* each other—forget why they're running, the door is never wider for our enemy, Satan, to enter and destroy what's been built.

There is a very real enemy who loves nothing more than destroying what God has set up for our good and His glory. Marriage is a beautiful picture of God's love for Christ and His bride (the church). We see this played out so many times throughout the Scriptures. God can and will use your marriage to bring Him glory and to do good in the world (Rom. 8:28).

> If you are in a marriage and you forget why you're running, the devil will pounce on your marriage like a lion until he's killed it.

But we can't forget why we're running. We *MUST NOT FORGET* why we're doing all this.

Being on mission with your spouse goes way deeper than loving the same type of movies, wanting to travel to the same countries, enjoying the same kind of food, or even working in ministry. Being on mission with your spouse means you both have your eyes on the prize of eternity, that everything you do in your lives, whether it be raising kids together, taking or leaving jobs, moving to new neighborhoods, or whatever—it is all for the same mission. It all has kingdom value.

It's all for the mission.

When our eyes are removed from this prize—and if you think they *can't* be removed, you haven't been married long enough—that's when we become like Pumbaa. That's when the lion catches up to us and begins to devour us. Listen, there's a real enemy to your marriage, and it's not the government, or your toddler or teenager, because neither of them truly listen to you. It's not some other woman who might catch the eye of your husband. It's not your budget constraints or your scheduling conflicts or your communication problems. It's Satan, and he wants to kill and destroy everything you've built together, everything God has started with you and wants to accomplish through you.

Aaron was right when he instantly burst my podcast dream with that one sentence. And he would be right again today if he told me the same thing. We truly both believe that everything we do must have kingdom purpose, or else it's not worth doing. That's our mission. Our eyes are on the prize, and as we complement each other along the way, we will run with endurance our race until we see Jesus face-to-face.

Our Prayer for You

Father,

We pray that you would strengthen and deepen the marriages of our friends, the readers. We pray their marriage would be Jesus-focused, Spirit-led, and used to displays the gospel of Jesus to everyone around. We pray that as each spouse serves, forgives, shows grace, and places courage in the other, You would be honored. Through hard times and sweet times, we pray this marriage would endure to the end.

Thank You for Your constant help, perfect wisdom, and immeasurable grace in each of our lives.

We pray all of this in faith, and in the name of Jesus. Amen.

Acknowledgments

We both know that putting any creative project out into the world takes a complete team effort. This book you hold in your hands wouldn't be in existence without the incredible people who have believed in this project as much as us and even more than us at times.

Over the course of our marriage, we have been surrounded by some amazing couples who love God fiercely and seek to complement each other in their marriages. We wouldn't be who we are without seeing healthy marriages lived out in front of us. Most of them, a decade or two ahead of us, have given us the courage to fight for a beautiful marriage. We won't list their names, but they'll know who they are. Thank you.

We both work with people who push us to be our best selves. Lyndsey and Brice, thank you for helping to free us up so that we can do all that we've been created to do. Thanks to the incredible Austin Stone staff and

Creative Team for constantly pushing us forward in creativity and in seeking Jesus with our whole hearts. The elders of The Austin Stone continually cheered us on, and kept us aimed at the Word of God as we wrote this.

Jenni Burke, our delightful and fierce Literary Agent, this will always be the book that came to life at a beautiful villa in Italy. You are a dream to work with. To all of our team at B&H, thank you for believing in this project from the get-go. Lawrence, Taylor, Ashley, Mary, Jennifer, Jenaye, Devin—you guys are rock stars!

We are basically the luckiest people in the world because we have so many fabulous friends cheering us on. Halim Suh, Greg Brazaele, and Zach Varrett, thanks for the feedback, critique and writing help. Aaron wrote most of this book in Marfa, Texas, with his side-kick Alex Espinoza. Thanks for the helpful conversations about singleness and marriage that formed many sections of this book.

Annie and Kyle Lent, Kevin and Leslie Peck, Halim and Angela Suh, Ross and Sue Lester—your love and excitement for this project are over the top crazy and humbling! Thank you!

Cayden, Amos, Deacon and Story, our house wouldn't be as fun without you, and our prayer is that this book shows the world something you've seen us live out every day. We hope you'll believe that God loves marriage, and desires for us to complement each other as we give our lives away because of the gospel. May that be true of all of us.

Jesus, we're still in awe that you would love us so perfectly and unconditionally. We've learned everything we know about marriage from You. Your love for Your Bride, the Church, is the kind of love we're aiming for in our own marriage. Let us reflect You in all that we do.

About the Authors

Aaron and Jamie Ivey live in Austin, Texas, where they parent four kids and do their best to change the world from right where they are. Jamie Ivey hosts the podcast, *The Happy Hour with Jamie Ivey*, has written some books, and will stop anything for some 90's hip hop. Aaron is a pastor at The Austin Stone, a songwriter, has written some books, and loves spending time cooking in the kitchen. Together they host the podcast, *On the Other Side*. They both believe that stories have such a huge impact on the world and are honored to share their story and lives with others.